"Wayne tells an interesting and ~~full story~~ ~~about~~ boy finding opportunity after surviving a difficult environment. With the support of his young bride he worked hard and made good choices. Then having achieved success, together, Wayne and Terry have set a good example for others with their generous giving back."
  – Earl Morrall, NFL Alumni, QB of Miami Dolphins 17-0 perfect season in 1972, Naples Florida

"Rich in imagery, this memoir unfolds like the petals of a morning glory in the kiss of the sun. An inspiring tale of familial devotion and decisions made which define different destinies for three brothers."
  – Carol Ann Erhardt, Romance Author, Columbus, Ohio

"A family torn apart by loss of their home and one young man who fought the odds, turning tragedy into triumph — and a life of giving back to others; an inspiring memoir for boys and girls in search of hope."
  – Mike Dennos, Founder of Chef Pierre Pie Company and Dennos Museum, Traverse City, Michigan

"I found myself immersed in the story, engaged in each episode, sharing Wayne's experiences and reliving some of my own. This story can reaffirm our youth of America's willingness to reward effort."
  – George Nemeth, retired attorney, owner of Nemeth Consulting group, New York City

"A brilliant written memoir. The book was special to me as I found myself re-living some of my own experiences growing up in Puerto Rico. A good example of how hard work and ethics can bring about success in this great country of ours."
  – Manny Hernandez, retired President of Colonial investor Services and Chairman of Broker-Dealer Advisory Group and Investment Company Institute, Hillsboro Beach, Florida

"From the cellar to the penthouse, an American dream,"
  – Jim Sullivan, Real estate Developer, Boston, Massachusetts.

"I thoroughly enjoyed the book and will recommend it to all my friends in Canada."
  – Tamara McIvor, Halifax, Nova Scotia

"Reads like a novel with more lessons than a bookcase full of self help books."
– *Rich Tarrant, Founder and Chairman of Marathon Health, former founder and Chairman of IDX.*

"Mr. Lobdell not only captures the broader meaning of childhood, but importantly preserves part of "Americana" culture that created the greatest nation ever known for its human bonding of diverse ethnicities. This is a personal testimony of how passion for life can create desired circumstances rather than becoming a victim of circumstances."
– *Robert Jones, Economist and Founder of Market News International and MMS International, Boca Raton, Florida*

"I couldn't put it down. The turning point in Wayne's career was when he met Terry."
– *Kevin Foley, Owner of hotels featuring conventions and entertainment in Gatlinburg Tennessee.*

"A poignant recall of a life journey, making one wonder what is it that builds spirit so different from one person to another."
– *Trish Fiebing, Director of Voluntary Programs, Traverse City Area Public Schools*

"Wayne Lobdell has an engaging writing style, which utilizes many descriptive analogies to make this work interesting for the reader."
– *Mike Tafuri. Retired VP of Proctor and Gamble, Cincinnati, Ohio*

"As a third generation Muskegonite from a foundry family, I was deeply moved almost to tears, laughed out loud and reflected on my own childhood"
– *Christine Cannon Bucher, Hillsboro Beach, Florida*

"A wonderful trip both thru Wayne's life as well as the reader's. I found myself reminiscing about events in my life that were similar and contrasting to the author's. A great journey."
– *Gerry Milot, Real Estate Developer, Burlington, Vermont*

Climb
From The
Cellar

**How One Michigan Kid,
Born in a Basement,
Found His Way
Up to the
American Dream**

A Memoir

by

Wayne Lobdell

WingSpan Press

Printed in the United States of America

Published by WingSpan Press, Livermore, CA
www.wingspanpress.com

The WingSpan name, logo and colophon are the trademarks of
WingSpan Publishing.

ISBN 978-1-59594-296-8 (pbk.)
ISBN 978-1-59594-331-8 (hardcover)
ISBN 978-1-59594-723-9 (ebk.)

First edition 2009

Library of Congress Control Number 2009923075

Contentment without prosperity
is better than
prosperity without contentment

I wrote these memoirs for my family and future Lobdell
generations. At the suggestion of those who have reviewed this
memoir, I have chosen to publish and give any profits to the
Boys and Girls Club of America.

The names of some of the people with whom I
crossed paths were changed.

To Terry
Jeff, Marty, Cherri and Greg

Table of Contents

Preface

Given a few minutes, I think I could have figured out each of their names. A thousand days and more I'd spent with these people. You get to know someone real well when you're in the same little one-room schoolhouse with them for seven hours a day, one hundred eighty days a year, from kindergarten through eighth grade. But I didn't have a few minutes; I was greeting them receiving-line style, one by one as they came into the room.

A half-century had passed since we had all been together, and yet, if not for the laugh lines, hairlines, and waistlines, the warm connection I felt with these people made it seem almost as if no time had passed at all.

And then, in came someone I expected to know on sight, but did not. She was a pleasant looking lady, nice smile. I looked at her, expectant. Intuitively, I could feel that she could read what I was thinking as my eyes met hers at the front entrance. Who is this? Why don't I recognize her? Something was familiar to me, but it was just a feeling of a shared past, and no name. Not right away anyway.

Everyone knew who I was of course, even if they didn't recognize my face right off. I had planned this reunion and was there at the door, wearing a sport coat, a tie, and a grin, with my hand out, welcoming each of them as they arrived. I detected a little disappointment in this mystery woman's voice when she said, "I got older. I'm Jacqueline."

I smiled and gave her a hug. I chuckled to myself thinking how I would never have been brave enough to give her a hug back in school when I had a crush on her that became increasingly intense from kindergarten to eighth grade.

Now what I felt for her, and for everyone in the room, was camaraderie. We had all survived Hoogstraat. Survived our teacher, Mrs. Lindgren. Survived our dirt road childhoods and parents who scratched out a living from their little farms.

I had tried to picture what each of them would look like as I planned the event. The only image I could conjure in my mind of Jacqueline was of a young girl in a brown ponytail. Back then, she looked just like a horse-crazy Elizabeth Taylor in the movie, National Velvet.

The same with another classmate, Janet Shook. There she stood, right in front of me, and I had no idea who she was until she said her name. For a time, even though we all took our schooling in the same room, she was the only other person in my same grade. A skinny little girl whose parents were more socially up-scale compared to the rest of us farm kids; the only kid in our country school with braces. "Wire teeth," my best friend Ronald and I would secretly call her. We had no idea what braces were until Janet showed up at Hoogstraat one morning wearing them. Tonight she had a lovely and genuine smile and looked younger than the rest of us.

All that time together, all those school days, and yet Ronald was the only one of my classmates whom I recognized right off. I had seen him once, fifteen years earlier. Ronald and I spent as much time together as we could back when we were kids. Not just school days, but weekends and days in the summer, too. They were not all good times.

In the past fifty years, I had tried to put Hoogstraat and the farm country I came from, and the road that led me away from that place and that life, behind me. And yet, here we were, all together again, exactly because I couldn't let go of that time. I wanted to find out what had happened to everyone from our little school. Funny how hard times are the ones we try to relive the most, whether we want to or not.

In planning this event, I had to make some phone calls to various branches of the Jablonski family, Jacqueline's maiden name, in the Ravenna, Michigan phone book. I found her on the fourth call. Jacqueline then helped me locate ten of our other classmates for this reunion dinner. Everyone was to be my guest for dinner at the Sundance Grill in downtown Grand Rapids. All ten came; some brought their spouses, some arrived alone.

The Sundance is one of my sons, Jeff's, restaurants. We used a private party room in the back for the gathering. After chit chatting for an hour, we settled down to dinner. I arranged the seating; my wife, Terry, on my left; Jacqueline on my right, next to her husband; Janet sat to the left of Terry. Ronald was seated with his wife in the middle of the right side of the U-shaped table. We were twelve in all.

I looked around the table. Fifty years gone by. How could that be? Fifty years ago I had never been to a restaurant. Fifty years ago my brothers and I were at the bottom of the pecking order at Hoogstraat; our farm was small and my brother, Lavern, was the class troublemaker. The Jablonski, Lane, Gilbert, Southland, and Shook names meant status back then. The Lobdell name meant trouble. I didn't plan this party to boast though; I just wanted to see them all again, somewhere I could feel equal; and I did.

I had fun, and I'm pretty sure they did, too. As it turned out, I wasn't the only one who wondered what happened to us all; they had all done their share of wondering about it, too. This was something we all shared, along with the memories of that place. We told stories we had all heard before and a bunch of new ones, too. They expressed condolences about my brother Gerald's recent tragedy; all having heard it on the news. No one asked about my other brother, Lavern. No one mentioned what had happened to Ronald and me in fifth grade.

Our conversation focused on happy times. Leave it to Ronald to tell everyone how I attempted to make a move on Jacqueline during a field trip when we were fourteen. Someone else brought up Mrs. Lindgren's hair pulling rages, but it only elicited some strained laughter. Those rages brought about fear fifty years ago and a little of that remained still; more intensely if your last name happened to be Lobdell.

I lay in bed the next morning thinking about how much I enjoyed the evening; having Terry with me. I was reminded of where I came from, my place in that school and the things that happened there, how my parents and brothers and I came to live on our little farm. I was also reminded of what happened to my Dad, my year in the hood; how close I came to entering the wrong world.

Like most people, I have lived in three different worlds; Birth to adulthood is the first; creating a career and family the second; and the third is retirement and the empty nest. How we maneuver the challenges of each of the first two worlds, the people we follow, our personal spiritual commitment, perseverance and generosity can set the stage for a long venue of rewarding years. Here's how I went from one, to the second, and finally my third world.

The Early Days

All Alone

Marion gazed upward, out the basement window and through the snowflakes blowing in the March wind. She didn't belong in a basement. That had not been part of the plan. Marion was just a deep breath over five feet, and strongly built on the outside, but even if few knew it, she sometimes felt delicate on the inside, like a crocus trying to make her way through the frozen drifts of white.

These lakeshore counties in western Michigan can hardly tell March from January, and the air wouldn't begin to smell like spring until Mother's Day. Maybe even later.

Marion was watching her husband, Howard, who was waiting at the edge of the road for his ride. A worn canvas jacket and last winter's gloves were all that protected him from the weather. He was always braced against something, and right now it was that wind. Straight from Lake Michigan and hard as liquid ice. It bent the spruce trees, flaked house paint, and rattled the storm door. People said it kept out the riff-raff. Transients from cities downstate left by October if they knew what was good for them. Marion and Howard were the furthest things from transients, though. They had come to stay.

A black Chevy pulled to the side of the road and Marion bunched her hand up into a fist. She was tempted to knock hard on the glass or yell out for Howard to wait, but stopped herself. He wouldn't hear her anyway over that wind. She felt a familiar jolt of pain and that could only mean one thing. The baby was coming and now Howard was leaving.

Only for the workday, but it certainly felt longer than that. Their first floor renter had already gone to work and Myrtle, her friend next door, was gone too.

It was before dawn on March 22, 1941 and, except for her two

1

little boys sleeping in their beds, Marion was alone. And about to have me, son number three. Marion, her husband Howard, six-year-old Lavern and two-year-old Gerald squeezed into the tight quarters of their basement apartment.

Where would the crib go? Where would the money come from to buy baby clothes and diapers? My parents were bringing a new person, a new Lobdell, into the world only to have it grow up in a basement.

Marion knew she didn't belong down there and neither did her babies and she was counting on Howard to move them up. Up in the daylight and out of the damp. Up into the open, where she could set a nice table and watch out a kitchen window with lace curtains while her sons played in a yard with a lawn. These were her plans for the future, and Howard's plans, too. Most mornings, she could almost taste the future and it was delicious to imagine their plans coming true. On this morning though, Marion was living very much in the present.

Lavern would be up soon, acting more rambunctious than usual because today was his birthday. Gerald had been up several times in the night, fighting a cold. Marion hurried into his room and put her hand on his forehead each time he coughed. A cold might start with just a runny nose, but she knew that it could creep deep down into the core of a child like roots from a poison weed.

Approaching Gerald's crib to check on him again, Marion looked up at the clock. It was just past 6:30 in the morning and she felt another jolt of pain. There was a bare space on the wall next to the clock for a telephone. For the first time, Marion questioned Howard's decision not to have one put in. It was too expensive he said, and besides, whom did she need to be calling? In the rare chance of an emergency, they could run next door and use the neighbor's. That chance didn't seem quite so rare anymore.

Everything about Marion was strong looking, from her workman-like hands to her coarse brown hair. She wore it short whether that was the fashion or not. The only round part of her, besides her pregnant belly, was her face and at just 5'1" a visitor might just look right overtop of her. Others considered Marion a nervous person, but that was just all of her energy, bundled tight and trying to get out. On its way to the surface, that energy made her limbs twitch and sprung her out of her chair at the dinner table a dozen times between the meat and the beans. It was energy all right, just not always channeled. An energy that started somewhere south of her neck and came out in her voice. Which she raised up out of her chest, up out of the basement and through the air towards Howard at every opportunity.

"Howard, I'm all alone the whole day. The whole day, Howard."

"Howard, Lavern's jacket is worn clean out."

"Howard, when can we get the boys some bikes?"

You wouldn't have known it by her tone, but this wiry man braced against the wind and the world was an improvement of gigantic proportions over Marion's first husband. That city-bred man had just disappeared one shining summer day, leaving her with their one-year-old, Russell.

Howard and Marion in 1934 wedding photos.

The day had been just like any other—crows sassed from the tops of the red pines, cicadas threw out their drowsy buzz and she put the coffee on just like usual. By the time it stopped percolating, she was a single mother. Common enough words today but "single" and "mother" were not spoken together in polite company in the 1930s.

It wasn't long before Howard saved her though. Saved her from the gossips and from a life harder even than this one. Marion was first introduced to Howard by her own sister. They dated for less than a year, married and then Howard adopted Russell. And just like that, the coffee was percolating again.

Marion and Howard had their first baby, Lavern, when Russell was five years old. The brothers would only have two years with each other. Husbands can leave in the daytime and sons can be taken away in the night, Marion knew from experience. When Russell was seven, he had a cold that reached into his lungs and turned into pneumonia. He was sick for just two days and died in his sleep.

Feeling another pain now, Marion moved to the couch in the middle of the room where she lay down and gazed up at the ceiling. The same ceiling that was really just the underside of their renter's floor. The ceiling she had watched Howard paint three years ago.

Her thoughts strayed while she wondered what to do if she had to have the baby all alone. Even though the little house didn't have a telephone or many modern conveniences at all, Marion calmed herself and tried to think instead about what it did have. Howard. The house had Howard.

Her laboring husband had done much of the work building the little Harvey Street home, even while he held down a full time job at the foundry. He had finished it just before winter set in, November 1938. The house was solid, if small, built with a wood frame and a pitched roof, thirty by fifty feet. The wind might bend saplings to the ground but it couldn't budge a house built by Howard Lobdell. He was the only man she knew that was just plain more determined than that wind.

Marion and Howard had bought a vacant lot for $250; Howard cut down the trees, burned the branches and chopped the wood into logs for firewood. He sold some of the firewood and burned the rest in the heating stove in the small apartment where they lived while Howard was building the house. The apartment was temporary, two miles away on Amity Street near downtown Muskegon.

Marion had thought of the basement as a luxury when he'd been building it. She'd since changed her mind. That's where they were living now, in the basement and there wasn't anything luxurious about it.

The original plan had been a sound one; she'd give him that. Her husband hadn't planned for them to live in the basement any more than she had. Howard would finish the basement and make it into an apartment, rent it out, and they would use the rental income to help make their mortgage payments.

No one wanted to live in a basement though, and after months of looking they couldn't find a renter. Howard counted his dwindling savings, closed his ears to his wife's complaints, and moved his family into the basement. He rented out the main floor of the house the very next week.

Like a lot of wiry men in their prime, Howard worked bigger than he was. Just 5'11" and 175 lbs, if his friends didn't know the saying "tough as nails" before, they knew it after they met Howard Lobdell. Thinning black hair covered a mind that worked just as hard as his body. He had the kind of skin that tanned in the summer and a face that chapped from being outside in the winter. Howard carried his lean muscular body with a slight foreword tilt. His somewhat large ears blended in surprisingly well with a handsome face. On the rare occasion that he got dressed up for an evening out, he'd usually wear a grey brimmed hat, giving him a Bing Crosby look.

The summer days of 1939 were long for the 30-year-old Lobdell. Men who tried to pack fourteen hours of work into a twelve-hour day looked like lay-a-bouts when compared to Howard. Off to work at 6:30 in the morning, then home to the apartment he and Marion were renting at 3:30 in the afternoon, if he wasn't working any overtime. A kiss on his wife's cheek and a quick bite to eat and then he'd walk or hitch a ride to the lot on Harvey Street where he was building their house. He'd work till dark and sometimes after, digging the basement, or as the project progressed, helping the carpenter.

Weekends were not weekends for Howard. His Saturdays started early in the morning too, Marion watching him as he left the apartment, carrying a brown bag with a peanut butter sandwich and an apple in one calloused hand, a bundle of tools in the other. His return trip home, sometimes after 8 o'clock, was the same routine, a two-mile trek in the dark. By the time Howard dragged himself back to their apartment, he had little energy left as he helped tuck Lavern in for bed.

Marion, then pregnant with Gerald, her second child with Howard, was just as weary. Her exhaustion came out in frustrating bursts. She wasn't happy with her long lonely days and would complain to Howard, especially on weekends.

"I'm going crazy in this little place, always alone, just me and the boys. We never go any place or do anything because you're always working. When you do come home, you just go to sleep. Work, work, work, and then a little sleep, that's all you ever do."

"I have to," Howard would respond. "It's the only way we can get a new house and get out of this apartment."

This exchange between the two of them became as much of a habit as Howard's foundry job and Marion's mothering. They repeated the same conversation a hundred times or more, with Marion eventually calming down and replacing her frustration with the image of a new house. A new house they would move into before Gerald was born. A house they would own. A house with a yard for the boys to play in and neighbors she could talk to. A home.

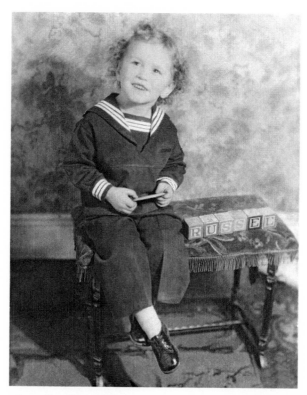

Russell - died of pneumonia on Jan. 22, 1937 at age 6

Baby Wayne spring 1941

Wayne in 1942 at about
18 months

Cellar Dwellers

And so that's exactly how it happened to be that the home that Marion dreamed of, that kept her going, turned out to be just the basement of their new house. Marion, Howard, and Lavern moved in the day before Thanksgiving in 1938. If Marion had been disappointed, she showed no signs of it on that day. She took the holiday literally and looked around instead for something to warrant her gratitude and found it, right next door.

Neighbors. She finally had neighbors. If Marion and Howard were Pilgrims in this new land, this little spot on the outskirts of town, Myrtle and Carl Vanderles were the locals who knew their way around and didn't mind sharing what they'd learned.

A cold beer was the first thing they shared, and it went as well with their offer of free labor as the Thanksgiving turkey went with mashed potatoes and gravy.

Though Howard worked the hardest, Myrtle and Carl helped them move their belongings out of the apartment and into Harvey Street. Not that it took long. All they had was a couch, a crib, a yellow Formica table for the kitchen and a few boxes of clothes. The most valuable thing they owned couldn't be lifted by a thousand well-intentioned neighbors. It was Howard's dream of owning a farm, and he carried that with him wherever he went, no matter how heavy it got.

It was with him when he dug the foundation with just a pickaxe, a shovel and determination. It was with him when he told his wife to hush her complaining, they'd be moving into the basement no matter what she said, and it was with him now while he worked on painting the walls. A light color would make them feel less like cellar dwellers, he hoped.

With the smell of fresh paint in their noses, surrounded by boxes, the highlight of the weekend was sitting down for that cold beer with Myrtle and Carl on Saturday night. Marion looked at her new friends in her new house. At her tired husband and her own swelling belly, seven months pregnant with Gerald. She took a deep breath.

"This is the first time in a year that we have sat down and visited," she said.

Howard smiled. He saw the same thing that his wife did: accomplishment. He was enjoying the break as much as she was. Plus, he loved to see her looking happy. If these new neighbors, friends now, made Marion happy, then they would be his friends, too.

The two couples exchanged background stories, talking until after midnight. Howard and Marion told the Vanderles how they once drove two hundred miles to Chicago and back in a borrowed Model A Ford, just to go to a barn dance. Carl talked about his office job and the little downtown apartment that he and Myrtle moved into when they were first married. Though it was almost a decade in the past, neither couple could keep their memories of the Great Depression silent for long. They both spoke of the stock market crash and the hard years that followed.

"The crash didn't bother me," Howard said. "The only stock my family had was a few cows and some pigs. We always had plenty to eat though. And wide open space. Nothing but the sound of crickets and birds and the rooster crowing."

Howard got quiet and felt far away for the next few minutes. The Vanderles didn't notice, but Marion did. She touched his arm to bring him back. "Gonna have my own farm someday," he said in a low voice, to no one in particular. "For Marion and for the boys."

Marion refused to let him be off by himself, even for a minute. They were socializing and he was going to join in whether he liked it or not.

"That's Howard's idea," she said loudly. "I'm not excited about living out in the woods where we'll never see anyone."

"We'll have neighbors," responded Howard.

"Sure," said Marion. "And what am I gonna to do? Ride a horse a mile to my neighbors? I can't even ride a bike. How am I going to ride one of those big animals?"

This sudden image of Marion in her housedress and apron, a baby on her hip and hard shoes on her feet, bouncing along on a plow horse gave them all a good laugh.

"She's got it all wrong," Howard said. "She'll learn to like the farm. And the boys? Well, they're going to love it!"

The Lobdells became good friends with Carl and Myrtle Vanderle.

Myrtle, a hospital worker, was there to help the doctor deliver Gerald two months later on January 10, 1939.

Then by the fall of 1940, Marion had one son who had grown to her waist and the other up to her knee and she was pregnant again. Pregnant with me. The basement apartment just wasn't going to work anymore, Marion told Howard. This time it wasn't a statement made from vanity or pride but one made using the laws of physics. Marion couldn't recite a single physics theorem or mathematical equation, but she knew how many people would fit in a 30 by 30 foot space and the answer wasn't five. The baby was going to outgrow her and they were going to outgrow that basement and this mother and wife, this young woman who hadn't gone to school past the eighth grade, knew for certain how both those equations would end, and at exactly the same time, too.

Howard had some money in his pocket these days, put there with nothing but an extra dose of his own sweat. Word got around that Howard Lobdell, that small wiry fella from Muskegon, the one good with tools, had dug his own basement in just a couple of weeks with nothing but a pick axe and a shovel. The few hundred dollars he'd saved from digging basements for hire and working overtime at the factory he'd already spent on a used 1933 Chevy.

Never one to spend good money on vanity, he knew it wasn't the bigger home that Marion wanted, but reliable transportation. Transportation that took him to and from any extra work he could land, whether it was at the factory or down some dirt road to a construction site. No more begging rides or spending half his workday walking.

He promised Marion that he'd look for a larger home. This one though would have two things that the house he built on Harvey Street did not: tillable land and a barn. Howard was still carrying around his dream of farming his own land with his sons, keeping it close but out of common sight, as if it were some shiny trinket that fate would just as soon crush under its boot heel as make real.

Howard set his sights on selling his Harvey Street house for a profit and buying a larger house as a next step to his eventual goal. So, staying in the basement "just a little longer honey" and living on a tight budget was necessary.

Two hours after daylight, Marion stared at a clock on the end table from the couch where she lay, listening hopefully for the sound of Myrtle's car. No sound came from next door though, and so with great effort she lifted herself from the couch. Her maternity smock draped down her body to her ankles, and even though it was cold outside the coolness of the painted concrete floor felt good on her swollen feet.

The pains continued, gradually becoming more frequent, while she changed Gerald's diapers, dressed Lavern, and fixed his breakfast. She bundled up the boys, hoisting Gerald on her hip and holding Lavern's hand tight while he struggled to march ahead of her on the way to the school bus stop. As the little group passed the Vanderle's house, she looked for Myrtle but the driveway was empty and the place was dark.

The school bus came, and she watched Lavern stride up the steep steps without so much as a look back at her over his shoulder. He was the independent one, always trying to leave her behind. Rushing away from her as fast as he could, even though she wasn't sure he even liked school. Back home it was just Marion and Gerald and the labor pains.

She put Gerald on the floor to play with some empty boxes and wooden toys that Howard had made and then returned to the couch. She knew what was coming. She'd given birth three times before and she knew. This baby had made a decision without consulting her: it was going to be born and it was going to be born right now.

Marion needed help and wanted to yell out but was afraid that her screams would scare Gerald. Would that be any way to introduce him to his new baby brother or sister? Though she wasn't always the best conduit for it, Marion wanted harmony in her household. She could at least start these two off with each other the right way.

Soon though she could hold it in no longer and just as she took a deep breath and prepared to scream, there was a knock on the upstairs door. Myrtle. Instead of a scream of pain, she let out a more practical command: "Help!"

Twenty minutes later, at 8:47 a.m., with the snow swirling outside and a kindly savior bearing the unlikely name of Myrtle, I was born.

Of course, this all comes not from my own memory but from other people's. My own first memories don't begin until after my father sold the Harvey Street home and we moved into a shabby-looking three bedroom on Manna Street, two miles away.

The day we moved in, true to his nature, my dad Howard set to work on the outside of the place straightaway, giving the wood siding a fresh coat of white paint. There wasn't a lot he could do for the green shingles flaking off the roof but replace them, which he did in time. The five of us lived in the upstairs of the house and used the downstairs for a playroom, a real upgrade from Harvey Street. The day my mother moved out of the Harvey Street apartment she said she felt like she had somehow been given the opportunity to see heaven while she was still alive to enjoy it.

"Goodbye, little dungeon!" she sang out, when they had packed up the Chevy with the last load of this and that. Our new home included a garage, a chicken coop, and a small tool shed on an acre and half of land. It wasn't a farm, but we were moving in that direction. Still struggling to save enough money to buy a real farm, this one and a half acre plot was a temporary substitute. To the surprise of some of our neighbors, my dad didn't wait for the real thing. He bought a milking cow, a pig, and some chickens.

I'm not sure how their parents felt about them but our animals sure created a lot of interest from the neighbor kids. Everyone who has ever had a pig knows how smart they are. As piglets they're like slippery bricks with minds as quick as an axe blade and set on just one thing – escape. Pigs can dig, burrow, scratch, and squeeze. They can run and dodge and jump and squeal. And they have a quality not seen in animals usually considered prey: they are patient. It's as if they have some way of knowing that a small hole in the pen today, will get a little bigger tomorrow and even bigger the next day.

On one of those next days, a Saturday I think, our pig got loose. My brother Lavern noticed Piggly Wiggly's pen was empty and alerted the rest of us. You have never seen a mom and a dad and three little boys become a team so quick. Our whole family spent hours that afternoon chasing Piggly Wiggly, followed closely behind for most of that time by our neighbors.

Back then there wasn't TV or video games or personal computers, and this was work, but it was entertainment, too. One neighbor, a big man we called Rollie Budd, showed himself to be surprisingly agile. He went after that pig like he was a linebacker and Piggly Wiggly was the quarterback. Rollie got his sack, too. He finally cornered and captured Piggly Wiggly when he made the mistake of scampering into a nearby garage.

I don't think our neighbors knew quite what to make of the young Lobdell family. Most of them were trying to escape their farm backgrounds and we were trying to make our way into one. Some of them liked us, I'm sure, and I think some others wished we'd move out to our farm as much as we did.

I did make one good friend, though. Benny Davids. He was eight and I was only four, and I would do whatever he asked, just to be included. I say we were friends. If you asked him, he'd probably say we were friends, too, sometimes. Other times, he'd just say he knew who I was, but that we were weren't exactly friends.

Bad Boy Benny

I can still smell that day. Even now, on certain dreary afternoons when the rain seems to drip endlessly, as if the sky wasn't really air and space but just an infinitely large leaky roof, if I pass someone smoking a cigarette, the moment instantly washes back. A smell and a feeling.

On sunny days, when people are naturally inclined to be cheerful, it is a memory almost forgotten. But not quite. I was four years old, and what makes that one memory so potent, is that it is my first memory of being at cross-paths with my mother.

It was a real roof, and not just the sky, that was leaking that day. The patched-up shingled roof on top of Benny David's garage. It was Saturday and it was raining, a tragedy for a four-year-old boy like me, who was just old enough to be allowed to play outside alone. My mother would keep an eye on me from the window, but it was still more freedom than I had ever felt. I liked it, and now this rain was going to delay my newfound bravado, if only for a couple hours. That didn't matter; patience was not something I'd learn until much later.

Benny, who was eight years old if he was a day, lived next door. By rights, he should have been one of my brothers' friends. Gerald was seven by then and Lavern a very grown-up seeming eleven, but as luck would have it, on that Saturday they were both otherwise occupied.

Gerald had rheumatic fever and had been banished to his bed for days; Lavern had a level of freedom I could only dream of and was off with some teenaged boys. Benny was mine.

Tending to Gerald had left my mother's defenses down, and she let me go to Benny's house to play. She only let me play with him because I'm sure she figured, 'How much trouble could a eight-year-old and a four-year-old boy get into, really'?

Water was dribbling down from that leaky roof about lunchtime. It dripped onto the ground in little pools all in a line. Outside, the sky grew a darker shade of gray, but I didn't notice. There was something inside the garage that had captured every cell of my attention. Benny had a crumpled up cigarette package with a few cigarettes in it. Not only that, he also had a pack of matches.

Benny got into a lot of mischief but I was young and didn't know that then. Even if by some measure I would've known it, I wouldn't have cared. I was like my mother in that way. In her longing for neighbors, for someone to connect with, for someone near by to share a story or a game or even just a wave hello to. I just wanted a friend.

Benny's first try at lighting the match didn't work. We were both kneeled down close together on the damp floor and he lit the match all right, but the recoil sent his hand and the little ember right down into a puddle. His second try flamed brightly. Then Benny placed the cigarette in his mouth, just like his dad, Mr. Davids, would do. He took a little hesitation puff and exhaled. The smoke mixed with the wet air and swirled around us as deliciously as white cotton candy. From the satisfied look on Benny's face, I thought it must taste that way, too. On the second attempt, he threw his shoulders back, sat up straight, lifted his chin in the air and inhaled. Even his gasping and coughing looked cool.

"That was good," Benny said when he got his voice back. "Give it a try."

I felt dizzy, and I hadn't even touched the cigarette yet. I felt an unfamiliar mixture of fear and curiosity. Most of all, I felt like making sure Benny thought I wasn't a baby. I followed his lead, took a small puff, and blew it out.

There was a car pulling into the driveway, but I didn't hear it. My mind was on the unbelievable fact that I had just smoked a cigarette. The sound of Benny's panicked voice put an end to my tingling daydream.

"It's my dad!" he yelped, shoving the pack of cigarettes into my hand. "Hide 'em!" My new friend walked casually to the edge of the open garage as if nothing had happened. As if we were both innocent. He glared at me and whispered, "Don't you tell!"

There was nothing else for me to do but go home. I scampered out into the drizzling rain and headed for my own house next door. As I ran into the front yard, my mother was just coming to the door to call me in for lunch. She had let me go to Benny's for just an hour, and I had managed to waste no time in finding a lit piece of trouble. I was sure at the time that she wasn't the wiser, but I should have remembered that she didn't miss anything. She knew Benny was a troublemaker, and so her guard was up.

Inside, my mother had a nice lunch prepared for me just like always, but as we settled down at the kitchen table, she did something that made my heart beat as hard as a thunderstorm. She began to sniff.

I held my breath as she leaned closer to me to take in the smell. From the look on her face, I could tell that lunch was suddenly and completely forgotten. She didn't smoke and neither did my father. The smell was foreign and obvious. She reached into my pocket and pulled out the evidence.

"My God, cigarettes. Smoking! You and Benny been smoking! Wait until I tell your Dad about this, four years old and you're smoking. Sit down in that chair and don't move until I get back. I'm going to talk to Benny's mother."

I was in big trouble now. My mom was surprised and probably disappointed and my dad would be mad, but I was more worried about Benny. I'd have to face him sooner or later. He'd be more than mad. He'd probably punch me.

"Do you want to stop growing up?" my mother asked me when she came back from the Davids. "Smoking stops you from growing. You will never get to be a big boy if you smoke."

Now, I was terrified. I pictured myself as an adult, but still my same four-year-old size. Everyone picked on me and I couldn't reach the steering wheel to drive a car. Just the idea of never growing scared me more than anything. I definitely wanted to grow bigger. I didn't like being the smallest kid in the neighborhood. It was worse than being punched, even by Benny.

When my father came home he levied his punishment. I couldn't play with Benny for a week. While my dad was looking, I acted duly contrite. When he turned his back, I relaxed. I liked that punishment. If I couldn't play with Benny, at least he couldn't punch me. And after a week, maybe he would have forgotten all about it.

Though he seemed ageless to me, one of those men who could be twenty or could be fifty, my father was thirty-six years old when my mother caught me smoking. His job was at Lakeys Foundry. He worked long hours and came home covered with black smut from the foundry. It was in his hair, on his lips, under his fingernails and in the creases of his palms. It must have been in his lungs, too, though he seemed unconcerned about it. Forty, fifty, sixty hours a week he breathed in the black smoke that churned out from the foundry's relentless furnaces. I had allowed one puff of smoke in, and was punished for it.

My father's job was important to the war effort; Lakeys Foundry, like many of Michigan manufacturers, was producing parts for the American World War II war machine. He didn't like his job. Money was the motivation. He was breathing in soot to someday be able to work in the fresh air and sunshine. He was saving up to buy a farm. For ten years he had been working in that dark and polluted foundry. Ten years of polluted air has filtered through his lungs, once as pink and unsullied as mine. Soon, he would have enough to make a down payment on a farm.

The black smut that was coating his lungs grew heavier and heavier every day. If he thought about it at all, it must have just seemed like the price he had to pay for a good-sized piece of tillable land.

Country Bumpkins

In the months before we moved to the farm, Sunday drives weren't just a quaint ritual for our family, they were a time to dream. After breakfast, my father would pack up the car with as many members of his growing family he could finagle into riding along with him and we'd make our way to the country twenty miles away.

On the drive, we'd pass the kinds of places that my father dreamed of owning and us kids dreamed of growing up on. Farms with endless pastures and fences as straight as if someone drew them with an ink pen. Farms with freshly painted chicken coops and big milking barns. Self-sufficient farms.

"Will we have cows?" my brothers and I would ask. "Will we have a horse we can ride? Will we have chickens and pigs? Can we get a dog?" We didn't know any better; farming to us meant animals we could play with.

"Maybe someday," was my dad's standard answer. He already did know better, and farming to him was a vocation, a living he could be proud of, a good life for his growing family. Plus, a whole lot of work.

A year later, in 1946, we finally moved to the farm. It was a small and not very well equipped farm, twenty miles from Muskegon and two and a half miles from Ravenna on a little out of the way plot on Squires Road. The place wasn't a bit small to my father though; it was a grand thing that he had finally made his own. It was a real farm.

My mother was less interested in owning land than in trying to replace the conveniences of the city, the few we enjoyed anyway, that were now long gone. First and foremost, indoor plumbing. To her constant annoyance, we had an outhouse and not a bathroom.

In the months leading up to the move, my father would make the drive from Muskegon to the farm every day after work and again on weekends. He was right that farming meant work. It was work just to prepare the place for his family to live in. This is what we were really doing on those Sunday drives. Not taking in the scenery, but fixing a window here, replacing a board there.

On several of these Sunday afternoon trips, even when my brothers and my mother declined to go along, I always got in the car. It was a rare chance for me to have my father all to myself, even if it was just for a few afternoon miles. My father spent so much time working that those rides were sometimes the only chance I had to see him all week.

Inside the intimacy of our old car, he would tell me stories. His stories were always about some member of our family, and listening to them made me feel safe. Grounded down to something bigger than my own little life. He was too busy or too tired to tell me these stories during the week at home, but in that car, his shoulders relaxed, and he talked.

Every time we passed through Ravenna and drove over the concrete bridge outside of town, he would say, "Here's your Grandpa's bridge."

My grandfather died in 1942 when I was still a baby, so I don't have any memory of him except these stories my father told me. They weren't very dramatic or heroic, but they were still living things to me. For a few minutes each week it was as if my grandfather was still alive, and just off doing his living somewhere else.

The bridge story was a simple one. My grandpa, Edward Lobdell, worked on building that little bridge. He was probably just a laborer, but my dad still proudly called the structure, "Grandpa Lobdell's Bridge" every time we drove over it.

Once, my father told me that as a child, he and his mother traveled over this same bridge in a horse drawn carriage. As they passed, his Mom would always say, "Here's the bridge your Pa built." Most of the people who drove over it had no idea that it not only spanned a river, it spanned generations.

One Sunday, my father and I arrived at the farmhouse to find an unexpected visitor. There was a small bird, just a tiny sparrow that had somehow gotten trapped in the attic. It flapped around in a panic until my father captured it in his bare hands.

Those hands that could string barbed wire and grip a whole bundle of roofing shingles could be surprisingly gentle when the situation called for it. He cupped the frightened bird inside of them and carefully handed it to me to hold. How small it felt. Its fragile breath and racing heart so close to my own. This tiny creature was going to be my first animal here on the farm. When I opened my hands to take a closer look, the bird flew away. My father tried to catch it again, but it escaped through an open window, probably the same one that it had come in through.

My little pet was gone and I couldn't help it, I cried. For his part, my father rested his big palm on the top of my head and didn't say anything at first, as we both watched the bird fly away.

"They'll be other things for you to take care of," he told me a little later. "Things that want to stay here."

Our project that day was to spruce up the outhouse, just until my father could add a real bathroom to the place. Though the outhouse didn't bother us kids much, my mother's feelings about taking care of her business outdoors was another story. She hated it. Her usual list of complaints now had another item added at the bottom.

"You're never home. I never see anyone. We never go anyplace," She would say. Then, as if mentally underlining this last addition she'd raise her voice every time she hissed the word "outhouse."

"It will not do, Howard," she told him, her hands firmly on her hips. "It simply. . . Will. Not. Do."

The outside toilet was unacceptable to my mother, would never be acceptable to her no matter the circumstances, and this time my father listened to her woes. An indoor bathroom was our first added renovation in late August.

The big event of the summer though wasn't indoor plumbing but the delivery of six milking cows. My brothers and I had them all named on the first day. I especially remember Bessie and Grumpy. To us, they were great big, four-legged, docile pets. To my father, they were proof. Proof that we were a family of real farmers. While my brothers and I wandered in the pastures with the cows, waded in the icy stream that passed through our farm, tossed sticks at the pigs to make them squeal, and hiked across neighboring farms to reach the woods, my father worked.

He was still an assembly line worker, breathing the blackened dust day in, day out at the foundry. He still drove twenty miles to Muskegon every day to put in his required forty to fifty hours every week.

My dad patched roofs, fixed fences, cut weeds, built feed bins, cleaned barns, and repaired milking stanchions. He only farmed on weekends and after dark while keeping his real job, the one that still paid the bills. By "farmed" I don't mean planting crops or harvesting them, I mean he got the place ready to be able to do that. I believe, though, that he had begun to think of himself as a farmer that summer. If someone asked him what he did, he said "farmer" and it wasn't a lie or even an exaggeration.

The best farm tool he had was our 1933 Chevy. It couldn't plow, till or haul much to market, but it got my father to and from his job in Muskegon, and then back to the farm. From time to time he would say, "Hope this old clunker gets me home from work."

He wasn't joking, and we all worried for him. I remember the sounds that car used to make, anxious sounds, as if it was worried, too. But I didn't care how he got there, I just wanted my dad to come home.

A One Room School

The summer of 1946 I had a frightful worry eating at me. Maybe I shouldn't have, but I did. That worry shadowed me all summer long, but unlike a real shadow it was just as present on rainy days as it was on sunny ones. My worry shadow followed me into the woods to play with my brothers, it followed me around when I did my chores, and it grew bigger and bigger in the twilight like some black and unnamed fur-covered creature whenever my mother, oblivious, tucked me into bed at night. For as long as I could, I kept it to myself. It didn't stop me from doing any of the things farm kids did in the summer– I still played in the woods, let the cows back into their stalls and hugged my mother, but it haunted me.

That fall, I knew, I was going to start school. I'd be walking there, and I'd be walking alone. I was five years old, I was going to be enrolled in the district's kindergarten class, the walk there and back was four miles long, and just the idea of it terrified me. My fears of what could happen anywhere down that rutted and dusty route that stood between the safety of home and the mystery of school usually involved hair and teeth and growling, and then me, flat on my back, fighting off some wolf-like monster.

In August, a week before the first day, my mother took me on a practice walk to the school, named Hoogstraat, and on our way home, I found that I could keep my frightening thoughts to myself no longer.

"Why do I have to be all alone? What if a dog comes after me? Why can't Gerald walk with me?" I asked her.

It was a simple fact of scheduling. Hoogstraat's teacher, Garnet Lindgren, taught thirty-five students, kindergarten through eighth grades, all in one room. Kindergarten was just a half-day, and so at noon, all of the kindergartners were excused for the day. Some kids were picked up by their parents; I had to walk home.

Hoogstraat, named in honor of the local farmer who donated the property, was a typical wood-framed, one-room country school building of the day. It had a single wood-floored classroom filled with rows of student desks, a coat room between the classroom and the entry door, and two bathrooms. At the front of the classroom was a bench for the teacher to sit on while she taught us our lessons. A single rope hung down from the ceiling, connected to a wrought iron bell she rang everyday to call us in from recess.

By the time us Lobdell kids were enrolled, Garnet Lindgren had been the teacher at Hoogstraat for a quarter century. She was teaching kids whose parents had been her students and she sure looked the part. Mrs. Lindgren ruled with a flesh-wrapped iron hand, a hand that would often smack a boy beside the head or jerk a girl out of her seat by her hair for the most minor infraction. Whispering to a friend would merit such treatment, or wiggling in our seats. Her pet peeve was the smell that wafted up from our shoes; most of us crossed at least one cow pasture getting to school and someone always brought in remnants of their missteps.

I joined six other kids, including my brother Gerald, in kindergarten. Our class of seven was the largest ever inflicted upon at Hoogstraat, which had been housing rural education since the 1920s, maybe even earlier. Even though he was older than me, when he was a toddler Gerald had been sidelined with rheumatic fever for two years, so he was beginning school as a kindergartner at the age of seven. My mother and Mrs. Lindgren had high hopes for Gerald though, and so he didn't leave in the middle of the day like the rest of our kindergarten class. The expectation was that he would hurry through kindergarten and first grade and catch up with kids his own age in second grade.

Our oldest brother, eleven-year-old Lavern, soon made Mrs. Lindgren forget my fear of walking home alone and Gerald's hoped-for educational trajectory. To say that Lavern didn't adjust very well to our new school was like saying a wolverine didn't like to be caged.

Lavern was silent when he was supposed to speak the answer to a lesson, and talked when he was supposed to be listening. He poked the other kids when Mrs. Lindgren's back was turned and hid their schoolbooks. Recess wasn't any better. He had so many scuffles with other kids that, more often than not, he spent what was supposed to be the best part of the school day standing in a corner, his nose pressed to the wall. Sometimes he was even escorted there by Mrs. Lindgren clutching a handful of his hair. Lavern was learning things, but it wasn't how to read history, or memorize spelling words, or figure out math equations.

My oldest brother's rabble-rousing behavior didn't do much for the Lobdell reputation as the new kids in town, either. Good manners, farm size, and being able to trace your roots in the area back a couple decades were the key factors of an unspoken, but obvious, class structure. As the new kids from a small farm, with one belligerent member of our clan and another whose education was delayed, my brothers and I were outcasts.

My mother wasn't always a sympathetic woman, but she was a practical one. Despite having to suffer through Lavern's almost daily trouble making and Gerald's hurried up lessons, she found a way to make my solitary walk home a little easier for me. She found me a fellow traveler, Juanita Kryderman, who was also in kindergarten and making a solo commute. She lived closer to the school than I did, so we only walked together part way, but that was enough to embarrass and satisfy me.

In front of my brothers and the other kids at school, I acted like it was an insult to be made to walk with a girl, but on the inside I was relieved to have any company at all. Having two older brothers meant I wasn't used to spending a lot of time alone, and anybody was better than nobody. Even if it was a girl.

Juanita and I walked the first half-mile together. I'd drop her off at her house and then walk the remaining mile and a half alone. My mother figured out a way to make that part of the trip not only safer, but something I actually looked forward to. She alerted all of the farmers who lived between the schoolyard at Hoogstraat and my front door that I would be walking home alone everyday around noon. By November, I knew not only the names of each one of those farmers, but their wives' names and their dogs' names, too. A foot of snow or more isn't unheard of by the first week of November in Western Michigan, and I had permission to stop at any of these farms to get warm. The imaginary devil dog I was afraid of turned out to be friendly, a pet that would run out to greet me, its tail circling in a happy windmill.

My favorite place to stop was the Mays. I didn't stop there out of necessity, but because I wanted to. The May farm was only about an eighth of a mile from my own house but I still stopped there almost every day. Not for the warm kitchen, but for the warm cookie. Mrs. May liked to bake and she often had a tray of cookies coming out of the oven when I knocked on her door. The sweet taste of that daily treat of warm butter and sugar made just for me by Mrs. May is probably one of the few joys I received during my early years attending Hoogstraat.

A single new student in 1947 resulted in a net enrollment loss of three; four graduated and one new kindergartner, Janet Shook, was added. As Gerald and I started first grade, Garnet Lindgren made it obvious that my brother wouldn't be skipping any grades. Instead, he was falling behind. Gerald probably had attention deficit disorder, though back then his behavior was just called "jumpy," or worse names.

Remembering how much trouble he had in the classroom, I think he might have had some other handicaps, too. Battling rheumatic fever for two years had left my middle brother fussy, difficult to engage, and easily distracted. Mrs. Lindgren's solution was to write him off as another Lavern, another problem Lobdell kid, and just assume he wasn't capable of following either her lessons or her rules. She didn't have a clue how to deal with him or my older brother.

Though I didn't know it, it was left up to me to lighten up our inkblot of a family reputation, as far as the Ravenna educational system was concerned. I think I was too young to feel anything but conflicted; I felt bad for my brothers, but embarrassed of them, too. Being their little brother had given me a new worry; that the other kids might not like me because I was a Lobdell.

"Say Give, Billy. Say Give."

A seven-year-old boy's choices of heroes were limited in 1948. They came from the news or the neighborhood or, more rarely, even from schoolbooks. The fall I entered second grade at Hoogstraat I didn't live in a neighborhood to speak of, and we were too far outside of town to get much news. I was a good student already but I still didn't spend any more time with my schoolbooks than I had to. My heroes were right in my own family, even though I didn't realize it at the time.

My dad and my brother, Lavern, loomed large in my life; they both seemed unafraid of anything that the world had saved up to throw at them. All the things, both real and imagined, that scared me they just flicked out of their mind like gnats, hardly worth more than a finger of time.

With me in school all day now and my dad so busy working on the farm, my hero worship was bestowed upon Lavern. He was the star of the most memorable event that happened in my second grade year. Like any memorable grade school drama, this one happened at recess.

Lavern and his sometime friend, sometime rival was another farm boy named Billy Steig. Lavern and Billy were like two sides of a cracked looking glass; nearly identical in size, both lean with a mean streak and already wrapped in wiry muscles. Lavern was fair-haired though and Billy was dark. One day they'd be allies, working together to scare the little kids and thwart whatever lessons our teacher, Garnet Lindgren, had planned for that day. Other times, they competed fiercely for status as the biggest, scariest, and toughest school bully.

One day, as the clock inched its way toward noon, the boys all wiggled in their seats, anxious for the softball game that would begin seconds after Mrs. Lindgren rang her desktop bell signaling our lunchtime recess. When she finally released us, we busted outside in a pack with Lavern and Billy tied for the lead and both headed straight for first base.

"I'm playing first," hollered Billy, as he elbowed his way in front of Lavern.

Lavern was having none of that. "No way, my turn for first base," he said.

"Nope, I'm first base," argued Billy.

"Then you're gonna have to fight me for it," countered Lavern.

With the whole school looking on, neither boy was about to yield. Billy responded to Lavern's challenge by giving him a hard shove. A weaker boy would have stumbled back, but not Lavern.

I squeezed my way to the front of the circle of kids that had formed around our little school's two rowdies. The other kids were yelling and urging their favorite fighter on, but I said nothing and just watched my big brother. He was my hero and I wanted him to push Billy Steig back even harder. Later, my brother was to disappoint me over and over, but not then.

Lavern gave Billy a two handed shove with everything he had and the fight was on. Lavern had Billy down, but he was no pushover and managed to wiggle loose and get to his knees. My brother moved in behind Billy, crafty as a well-thrown knuckle ball, grabbed his left arm and pulled it up behind has back, all the way up to his neck. Billy dropped face first to the ground, his mouth touching the dirt. "How you like my arm pile driver now, Billy?" Lavern taunted. Lavern had Billy in a wrestling hold that they both had learned watching wrestling on television at Billy's house.

Some of the other kids loyal to Billy groaned, but not me. I was enjoying seeing my brother on top. Then came the ultimate humiliation.

"Say 'I give' Billy, say 'I give'," Lavern bellowed into Billy's ear.

"Not givin', Slobdell! Not givin'," Billy retorted, using every bit of grit he still had in him to lift his face above the dirt.

"Better give Billy. I can break your arm." Lavern sat on Billy's back, determined to hold his advantage.

"Ain't givin', let me up," Billy commanded.

Everybody, even me, Lavern's biggest fan, cringed when he pushed Billy's arm up and we heard the snap.

Billy cried out something terrible and Lavern let go and jumped to his feet.

"Sorry, Billy, sorry! I didn't mean it," Lavern pleaded, "It was an accident."

Not even I was buying that line. Even as a little second grader I knew this was no accident. My big brother was gonna get it now. As if on cue, Mrs. Lindgren came running outside to see what the commotion was about. She took one look at Billy and told all of us to go inside and sit down in our seats. She put two eighth grade girls in charge of the class while she took Billy to the hospital in her car.

I cringed when Mrs. Lindgren returned. I could only wonder about what Lavern must have been feeling. We all knew what was coming, especially him. Flames of hate shooting from her eyes, she marched down the aisle, hands clenched into fists, toward Lavern. He braced himself by scooting down in his seat, arms pressed against his body. She grabbed my hero by the hair, yanked him out of his seat, and dragged him to the front of the class. Now it was Lavern's turn to yell out in pain.

Our teacher wasn't big, but years of disciplining rangy farm kids like us had made her strong. She yanked my brother to and fro like a champ on the wrestling shows he liked to watch so much. I wouldn't have been surprised to see a clump of his scalp fly off his head when she was finally through.

"You're just a heathen, a no good for nothing!" She spit. "You'll never be good for nothing! You're just a no good for nothing Lobdell."

She might have been aiming her insults at my brother, but it felt like she was talking to me, too. We didn't share much back then, Lavern and I, mostly because he was so much older, but we shared a name. A name I had always been proud of. I can still sometimes hear the sound of her voice shouting "No good for nothing Lobdell." Our teacher might have been talking just about Lavern, but I was feeling all of his pain, all of the humiliation, the embarrassment.

"Now go home and don't come back to my school," were her parting words for Lavern as she whipped him toward the door.

Mrs. Lindgren didn't end up having the final word on Lavern's education, though I was certain she would have liked to. My oldest brother did return to school to finish his final month of eighth grade. An accomplishment that didn't pacify my mother. She was still distraught over the whole incident. My other hero, my dad, didn't seem too concerned about any of it. "The boys are going to have a few scraps," I overheard him tell my mother.

That was like him, though. He didn't always think fighting was bad. When we'd fight amongst ourselves, my dad was kind of like me, standing in that circle of kids and just watching. He was curious to see who could 'lick' whom, even when the fighting was among his own boys. Whenever my brother Gerald and I would get into a fist fight, my dad would watch for a while before breaking us up. He wanted to see who was winning. I was usually in retreat.

Harvey Street home in Muskegon - built 1930s.
2007 photo.

Howard, Marion, Laverne, Gerald, Wayne in spring 1948.

Living Off The Land

Pouring On The Flour

Back then, danger hid in the most unexpected places. Having finished with eighth grade, not to mention with Mrs. Lindgren and Hoogstraat, my parents decided that Lavern should become more involved in the farm. My dad worked on other farms in the area, sometimes for pay but usually for trade in labor. Farms are like giant pits that hours of work disappear into and Lavern's help would fill those empty spaces. Now that my oldest brother had no use for school, and school felt the same way, my parents had decided that Lavern would do the same as my dad. Work on our farm and other farms, too. His first day at it proved not to be a very good beginning.

First thing that morning, Lavern and my dad went down the road to Louie Steinberg's farm. Mr. Steinberg wanted an addition on his barn so that he could add to his dairy herd and my dad and my brother were doing most of the hammering and nailing. Somehow, a board that had been placed wrong and pried off for use later was left on the barn roof, nail side up. While the men were busy working, it fell from fifteen feet up and landed squarely on Lavern's head. His skull was slashed wide open, and blood spurted out across his face and onto the ground. Not much could damage Lavern's hard head, but tough as he was, he was still no match for carpenter nails to the skull and crumpled to his knees, screaming. Mr. Steinberg ran for his house, returning moments later with a bag of flour.

"Keep pouring this flour on his head till we get there," he told my dad. Together they carried Lavern to Mr. Steinberg's pickup truck and sped off on their panicked journey to the hospital. Mr. Steinberg drove while my dad did exactly as he was told, covering Lavern's bleeding head in white dust, which slowly turned into a pink-colored paste.

"We gotta go to Sparta. Better help there than in Ravenna," Mr.

Steinberg decided, as he raced down the driveway. Sparta was nine miles away.

"Oh God don't let me lose this boy," my dad cried to himself. Tears of fear ran down his face and dripped onto Lavern's head, dripping into the pink paste. "We'll be with the doctor soon. He'll make you better," my dad said over and over as Mr. Steinberg pressed on the gas and ignored every stop sign in their path. He drove with one hand on the steering wheel and the other on the horn.

My dad said later that it was the longest nine-mile ride of his life. He prayed for Lavern to remain conscious and his prayers were answered. Lavern was awake all the way to the emergency room, though I'm sure it hurt so bad he probably wished he wasn't.

A nurse shaved his head and the doctor sewed in thirty stitches. The flour, he said, had saved Lavern's life. Saved it for battles yet to fight and difficulties yet to bear, as it turned out. Lavern was headed for uneasy times that couldn't be solved with just a bag of flour and a fast drive. In the ensuing years, my father would often wonder how much internal damage was done to Lavern from those nails.

Getting Some Upgrades

That spring, I looked out the window one bright day and saw that my dad had become his dream. He had become a farmer.

Not a man who imagined holding his own soil in his own hands, who imagined feeling the heat the dirt gave off in the morning, but a man who actually did those things. It seemed to me like one day the view from our front window was flat and vacant, and the next day it was lush and profitable.

Up from our square of hard-fisted land came sweet corn, strawberries, raspberries, cucumbers, and string beans. As far as I could see, everything was green, and later when it was time to harvest, those same things turned a vibrant yellow, pink, and red. What started out as seeds in my dad's hands ended up on our kitchen table at dinner, or inside glass jars preserved for the winter, or on their way to be sold at the local farmers market.

The rest of us felt like a farm family as soon as homegrown sweet corn appeared, as if by magic, on our dinner plates, but not so my dad. It was making a sale at the farm market, and not the overalls or the worn work boots or the fresh vegetables at meal times, that gave him his identity. And, he made sure he had the right go-to-market equipment, even if it was jerry-rigged. My dad bought a buggy axle at an auction, purchased some one-inch by four-inch boards, and framed them out into a six-foot by ten-foot box he used as a hauling trailer.

On most occasions, Dad would go off to the market with Lavern while Gerald and I suffered the indignity of staying home with our mother. On the rare times that we were invited along, we were thrilled. We wandered throughout the market and were almost always treated to a Popsicle. With the morning sun as our enemy, my brother and I still licked those Popsicles slowly, trying to make them last as long as we could. When they were gone, we chewed on the sticks, grinding out the last of the sweet orange or grape or lime. Gerald sometimes even sucked on his sticky fingers, though I wouldn't and wiped my hands on my pants instead.

Just like at school, there was a pecking order at the farm market.

And, just like my brothers and I had fallen far short of the top of it inside Hoogstraat, my father did so here. The bigger the farm, the better, richer, and smarter the farmer, went the conventional wisdom. Nobody ever talked about this unfair system of judging each other, it was just known and universally accepted. Someone had to be on the bottom and that was us Lobdells. Someone had to be on the top and that was Wally Wagoner.

Wally was a big time fruit farmer with acres and acres of fruit trees and berry bushes and all manner of vines and watermelon patches. His trees were old and healthy, his vines were perfectly staked and his patches were weed-free and so heavy with watermelon it looked like he was growing enough green basketballs for every high school in America.

Wally's booth at the farm market was something to behold, and Gerald and I were more awed than jealous. There were baskets of Red Delicious apples – my favorites and hard to grow, according to my dad. There were quarts and quarts of strawberries, and of course, those watermelons. Approaching his booth one day, I was struck silent by the abundance of Mr. Wagoner's display, but my brother somehow found his tongue.

"Hello Mr. Wagoner," he said. "We're your neighbors. I'm Gerald, this is Wayne."

Wally Wagoner was not a big man, and so his ears weren't so far up above my brother's small voice that could reasonably pretend that he hadn't heard him. There weren't any customers in his booth at the moment, so he couldn't pretend we were interrupting a sale. He just pretended we weren't even there. Neighbors or not, he pretended there weren't two small boys in worn but clean clothes standing in front of him, trying to make his acquaintance.

I'd have been wearing black boots with soles that were half worn through, a flannel shirt with holes in the elbows, and corduroy bib overalls tethered at the knee, but underneath I still had some pride. Mr. Wagoner didn't need to pretend at all; we might have been young and we might have been little, and he might have been absolutely silent, but we knew exactly what he was telling us.

Being snubbed by a neighbor was about as irritating as getting a sliver in your gum from chewing on those Popsicle sticks. It hurt, and vexed us something awful, but at least the pain didn't last long.

Our farm might not have been as elaborate as Wally Wagoner's, but it was growing.

Our milking stock of cattle grew from a herd of six to a herd of thirty. With Lavern's help my dad added a silo, a milk house, a corn shed and some basic farm equipment. And my dad started spending more time with us, even if it was just to pile on the chores. He was around the farm all day now because he had finally been able to quit his job at the foundry.

That didn't slow down his work schedule any though; he used every minute that he would have been at the foundry to work even harder on our farm. For the few hours a week he wasn't farming our land, he was working at one of our neighbor's farms.

My dad might not have had thirty-year-old trees that produced bushels of Red Delicious like Mr. Wagoner, but he knew this first rule of farming: Labor is more valuable than money.

At harvest time, you could have all the money in the town's bank right in your pocket, but if you didn't have enough hands picking, it didn't mean anything. He knew that he might not be at the top of the pecking order, but as long as he had men to help him when he needed them, he didn't really care. And so, rather than take pay when he worked on other men's farms, he waited for return favors at harvest time. He made sure that his labor was spent in the right places, too. He gladly helped out at the larger farms and the men who owned them would help out at ours, and bring their big and efficient harvest equipment along with them.

All Howard Lobdell had in those first years on the farm were his muscles and his smarts, but he used them to get other supposedly better, richer, and smarter farmers to drive up to our little place on their tractors and their threshers and their tillers, ready and willing to work.

All this made my dad as happy as Mr. Green Jeans. My mother, on the other hand, was, as usual, another story. As progress was made on the farm, my mother became indignant about wanting to upgrade the house. My dad would listen to her in his quiet, measured way, nod his understanding, and then usually say no. He knew that money put into the farm would bring a return; money put into the house would only bring a little comfort or convenience.

Because of this, my parents had frequent arguments about what we could and couldn't afford. But whenever he said, "I still got payments to make on this farm," it would always win any argument. Eventually the upgrades came, but always with used goods my dad found, scavenged, traded for, or bought at a discount.

I was aware of how hard my dad was working, I watched the growth of our farm, and listened to the arguments between my parents, but I spent most of my time with Gerald. We built hay forts in the barn, pretended that sticks were either guns or bow and arrows, depending upon whether we were cowboys that day or Indians. It was a good thing Gerald and I had each other because we didn't see much of Lavern. He had become an acolyte of my dad's and on the few hours a week that he wasn't working, he'd be off with his mismatched and rough group of friends.

Life was hard for all of us, but I think that it was especially hard for Lavern. He had inherited my dad's work ethic, but not his patience and good sense, and one without the other turned out not to be much help. My dad paid him for his work and Lavern also made money working for neighboring farmers, but he spent his money as fast as he made it. He'd devote hours tilling, planting, and harvesting in our fields, and whole days cleaning out our barns, repairing fences, and walking back and forth to his jobs at other farms, but still never had anything but exhaustion to show for it. It was as if all that working had worn holes in his pockets and in his judgment.

I knew from experience that the holes were real, at least the ones in his pockets. I wore his hand-me-downs and I lost three nickels I earned by picking strawberries for another of our neighbors, Mr. May. I don't think that's the way Lavern lost his money though.

He regularly left his bed unmade, got into fights with other boys, came home late or not at all, and would work for money but then forget to do his chores. He'd leave with friends and then not return until the middle of the night. My mother was an expert at whining and hollering about Lavern's behavior, but not so accomplished at doing anything about it. My dad, tough as he was on himself, thought that us boys should know how to behave, and should show our good character of our own accord, and didn't like to discipline his kids. I can't think of any time he took a stick to Lavern and only once that he laid in hard to Gerald and me. Lavern might have deserved it more than a few times, but we deserved at least that once. That's because fire was involved.

If you ask boys why they like fire, they'll probably just answer "because" and it's as good an answer as any. Because it's powerful, because it's dangerous, because it's forbidden, is what they mean. One chilly fall day, Gerald got it into his head to drain some gas out of the farm gas tank into a pail. He and I carried the pail to the edge of the large pond near the barn. Next to water is a safe place to light gas, right? Back then if you asked my brother and I why we threw a lit match into a pail full of gasoline, "because" is the answer you would have gotten.

We lit the gas, expecting nothing more than a warm little fire. Maybe we'd throw in a few handfuls of pine needles and dry grass and watch it crackle and glow. Maybe we'd wave a long stick through the flames. Maybe we'd just hold up our palms to the heat. None of this happened, though. The flames jetted straight up ten feet or more with a loud whoosh. They were instantly high enough to be seen from the house. High enough to draw the attention of our dad if we didn't do something, and do it right now. That something was kicking the whole burning pail into the pond. Water, we figured, would put out the fire, destroy the evidence, and keep our parents in that welcome state of oblivion.

I didn't know this then, but I sure know it now. Gasoline floats on water. This was a hell of a way to learn a science lesson. Suddenly, it looked like our whole pond was on fire. Gerald and I panicked and ran away, straight into my mother and dad, who had seen the undulating orange blaze from the house. On their faces were the looks of panic and loss. They were sure that the barn, or the house, or the fields would catch fire. The four of us stood silent and watched and waited. There was nothing else for anyone to do, even my dad. The water that we could have used to put out the fire was burning. As we watched, the flames quickly burned themselves out and all that was left was a greasy floating rainbow.

I looked up at my dad, half expecting or at least half hoping for him to say something like, "Its OK boys. No harm done." Instead, the fire that burned itself out on the pond had leapt into my dad's blue eyes.

There wasn't any harm done to the farm, but Gerald and I both saw harm coming our way in a hurry. Dad pulled a stick from a willow tree and came after us with the vengeance of a man who almost lost everything. Revenge wasn't part of his nature though and when he caught us, he just swatted us halfheartedly. I still cried from the shock of it. Howard Lobdell could put up with a lot from his boys; fighting, missing chores, staying out late but this was something else entirely. Even his boys couldn't be immediately forgiven for endangering Howard Lobdell's farm.

Danger for Grandpa

Once Dad moved us all to the farm, it was as if we had hung out a shingle in the front yard that read, "Hotel Lobdell." You'd think a city address with the promise of at least a few modern conveniences would have been more inviting to our aging relatives than a run-down farm, but not so. Maybe it was because they felt reassured back in the kind of rural outpost where they spent their own childhoods, but I can't ever remember when we didn't have some relative living with us.

Dad was always worried about having enough money, and his scrimping was legendary, but he wouldn't save money by refusing someone a home. Somehow, he still managed to pay all of our household bills the day they were due and not a second after. I knew this because he and my mother would talk about it often, and I overheard.

A whole lineup of Lobdells, DeWilders, distant relatives and people of no blood relation but in need of a temporary home walked up our front steps and were treated to a single hot meal or many, and given a bed for the night, the month, or, in the case of my Grandpa DeWilder, the rest of their lives. Never once did my dad hesitate to take someone in.

Besides my Grandpa DeWilder, my dad's mother, Grandma Lobdell, blind with cataracts since she was just forty-five, stayed with us for awhile. My dad's dad died of a heart attack before we ever moved to the farm, but not before he got to know me even though I was only a year old. He knew me pretty well in that short time, too. Grandpa Lobdell gave me a nickname; he called me "Proudy" because even at that age I walked around with my chest sticking out.

In 1946, Grandpa DeWilder, my mother's father, moved in. He lost his wife in 1942, the same year Grandpa Lobdell died, but Grandma DeWilder had a much more painful end. She accidentally swallowed a piece of glass from a broken jar while canning peaches. It cut her up inside and she died a few days later.

By the time he moved in with us, Grandpa DeWilder was blind, skinny, and seemed as ancient as the men in my school history books to me. His clothes hung off him like a sheet draped over a skeleton. The man was an anomaly of human anatomy because he was far too skinny for someone who liked to eat the way that he did. Especially desserts. He'd eat the pies and cookies and sheet cakes the neighbors brought over and his sweet tooth became a part of local mythology. Every cook worth her flour sifter likes to see the smile on an old man's face, and my mom soon found out that he especially like strawberries. He devoured her strawberry jam on toast and followed it up with a plug of chewing tobacco.

"Marion, where you at?" he'd call, if he was hungry and couldn't find my mother. "Can you get me some of your jam on toast?" If he ran out of toast or tobacco, we'd steer clear of him because we knew he was about to get cranky.

One Sunday in June my mother was busy planning one of Grandpa DeWilder's favorites for dessert, strawberry short cake. My mother was not all that accomplished in the kitchen, but she had a few tried-and-true recipes that were always sure winners with us, and one of those was baking powder biscuits. Her strawberry shortcake bore little resemblance to the dry, bowl-shaped sponges packaged in cellophane and sold today in grocery stores. She used a warm biscuit cut in half and buttered, with a topping of sugar-sweetened mashed fresh strawberries ladled on top. And, if we had it, fresh whipped cream from our own cows was the crowning touch. One bite and you felt like summer could surely last forever.

I think that freshness was the reason that food tasted so good on the farm, and on that day my mother had sent us boys out to the strawberry patch to pick the berries. Dad was at the back end of the farm, busy with the never-ending job of repairing a fence. Barbed wire didn't care that Sunday was supposed to be a day of rest.

My brother and I were bent over picking as fast as we could, mouths watering already for dessert even though we hadn't had dinner yet. Our hands were stained red when we heard my mother screaming.

"Pa, Pa, don't move! Stop, Pa, stop!" She was screaming at her maximum lung capacity and maximum volume which, on many previous occasions, had impressed not only us kids and my dad, but the neighbors, too. The back entrance of our house had a porch about four feet above ground level with no railing. A handrail around the outside was just one of those improvements my dad hadn't gotten around to yet.

When I looked up from berry picking, I saw one object moving very slow and another moving very fast. Grandpa DeWilder, barefooted, had wandered out that back door and was walking straight toward the edge of the porch. He was probably looking for my mother, or for some toast and jam, or some chew. My mother was running for all she was worth, across the berry patch toward the house, and screaming as she ran.

"Go back, go back!" she screamed to Grandpa. His selective hearing picked a very bad time to click off and he just kept edging foreword, one foot out like a pole in a cloudy river.

My brothers and I thought for sure Grandpa was going head over teakettle off that porch, so much so that we could almost hear his brittle bones breaking to bits, but we were too far away to do anything about it. My mother didn't care how far away we were though, didn't care that she had short legs, a dress on, and a berry patch between her and her endangered father. She covered the space between the berry patch and the house in seconds and crashed up the porch steps like a one-woman stampede. She grabbed Grandpa by the arm and gently guided him back in the house. While we watched in awe, the old man seemed to think the whole episode was funny.

"What were you getting so excited about?" he asked my mother. "I was feeling for the edge with my toes."

By the time my dad made it to the front of the house from the field, all he could do was shake his head and comment on the decibel level of all the hollering he had heard coming from my mother.

"You were so loud, people in town are still covering their ears."

Goodbye, Grandpa

Grandpa wasn't always joking, though. He could get mean when a bad mood struck him. His fragile health and blindness was at the root of this, I'm sure. I remember Grandpa Evart DeWilder, better known as "Baldy" because he lost all his hair at a relatively young age, as a frail and sickly little man. "Pa," as my mother called him, was often sick with colds or stomach troubles. My dad thought he'd brought some of his troubles on himself.

"Stop chewing that damn tobacco and you would feel a lot better," my dad would tell him.

"Nope Howard, been chewing this stuff all my life, ain't stopping now," Grandpa would respond, and then he'd spit a brown stream into a bucket.

Pale faced, slim and shrunken down to just five foot five from a healthier and respectable five foot eight, Grandpa DeWilder might have been blind, but my brothers and I can attest that he still had some wicked moves with his cane. As the youngest and smallest in the family, at only eight years old Grandpa favored me and threatened to take his cane after my brothers when they picked on me.

"You boys leave him alone, 'er I'm going to whack ya!" he would yell out, cane waving in the air, whenever he heard me getting the worst of it from Lavern or Gerald. If it were Lavern that Grandpa was yelling at, my oldest brother would leave me alone and turn his attention on the old man. He'd sneak around behind Grandpa's back and say "Boo!" real loud then get to heck out of the way, just in time to avoid Grandpa spinning around with a wicked swipe of his cane. The cane would break air harmlessly, high enough up where it couldn't have really hit Lavern or anything else.

Looking back, I don't think he ever had any intention of striking anyone with that cane except maybe once. That time, he was going for something solid, like Lavern's head. It was the ninth inning of a Detroit Tigers-New York Yankees baseball game. The game was tied and Grandpa's favorite Tiger, George Kell, was at bat. There was a full count and Lavern tiptoed up and turned off the radio. I thought Grandpa was going to spit steam instead of tobacco juice he was so mad. I was listening to the game with him and I turned the radio back on as Lavern ran out of the room. With a click, George Kell grounded out and Grandpa's hated Yankees won again. He blamed the loss on Lavern.

Another Sunday morning, this time in September of 1949, my brother Gerald and I, sleeping in our upstairs bedroom, were awakened early by the sound of my mother's shouting. Grandpa DeWilder was in trouble again but this time there would be nothing humorous about it.

"Howard! Howard! Pa is hardly breathing!"

Dad had just left the house for his morning chores, and was heading for the barn. It must have been before 6.

Grandpa had not been doing well for the past few days, sick with another cold. This one was bad, and he couldn't seem to shake it. When he came back to the house Dad took one look at Grandpa and then ran out again, and across the street to use the neighbor's phone. He called the local Ravenna doctor. By the time my brother and I got out of bed the doctor had already examined Grandpa and was talking in low tones with my mom and dad. My mother was crying.

A few hours later, Aunt Grace and Aunt Evelyn arrived. They all gathered around Grandpa in his bedroom. I was only eight years old, and nobody told me what was happening, but I knew what was up and so did my brothers.

Grandpa Evart DeWilder was born a triplet on July 18, 1868, in Chicago, Illinois, the year that General Ulysses S. Grant became President. One of the triplets, a brother, died at birth. Evart and his sister, Kate, survived and were always referred to as "The twins."

In his late teens, Evart hitched a boat ride from Chicago across Lake Michigan to Muskegon, Michigan. There he was hired on as a laborer in a cigar factory and he worked there most of his adult life. He married Ricky Leifers in 1904. Ricky gave birth to twins in 1909, but the babies had a tougher time than Evart's long ago brother did and they both died, one at a month old and one at two months. Then the DeWilders had a son, Albert, and a daughter, my mother, Marion and then two more daughters, my Aunt Grace and my Aunt Evelyn.

Evart lost his sight in 1940 and had to quit work. There wasn't any call for a blind cigar-maker. . His wife Ricky died in 1942. She was the one who swallowed the piece of glass. Evart lived alone for five years or so, his son and three daughters taking turns checking in on him. In 1947, Evart "Baldy" DeWilder moved in with our family in Ravenna.

Grandpa died that Sunday afternoon, September 25, 1949. He missed hearing on the radio that the Boston Red Sox had moved into a first place tie with the New York Yankees. If he had lasted a few more weeks, he wouldn't have been happy about the outcome of that series. The Yankees won another World Series that year.

The aunts covered Grandpa's body with a sheet, and he was taken away in a black and shiny hearse. But when my brothers and I returned home from school Monday, Grandpa had returned. His body was on display in a casket in our living room. His cane was leaning against that shinny wooden box, and photographs and flowers surrounded the casket. Many family and friends came to our house to look at Grandpa. They all said that he looked good, but I didn't know how they could think that. I thought he looked spooky. My brother Gerald and I took a long time getting to sleep with the picture in our heads of Grandpa DeWilder lying down there in the living room.

"What if he wakes up?" I asked Gerald in the dark.

"He will come up here and hit Lavern with his cane," Gerald decided. And with that solemn prediction, Gerald got out of bed, walked across the hall to Lavern's room, and told him, "Baldy is going to get up in the night, and come in here, and hit you with his cane."

Lavern was tough but this rattled even him. He jumped from his bed and lunged at Gerald, who dashed back to our room and dove under the covers with me. Lavern came in and gave Gerald a couple good pokes through the covers, but he didn't hit hard. His heart wasn't in it.

That was the last I remember of Grandpa DeWilder. After the funeral my dad said "I'll miss that little old bugger," but I'm sure he didn't mind having one less mouth to feed. Although, as we soon found out, Dad couldn't say no to any family member in need.

The Chum Challenge

Ma was both the shopper and the reader in our family. Much to the frustration of Dad, sometimes she would even combine these two activities to surprising effect. Ma would read about a cure-all in a magazine, or see a pair of shoes in a newspaper advertisement, or sit for hours in the evenings with the Sears catalog, and then days or weeks later a package would arrive on our doorstep. Inside would be whatever amazing product that had caught her fancy. One winter day when I was eight, the package that arrived contained something unimaginably wonderful. Not a dress pattern or a headache tonic, but a puppy.

Ma had read a magazine article about Old Fashioned English Shepherd dogs and decided that our farm should have one. She ordered the dog from the magazine and had him shipped right to us. We took one look at his fuzzy head and, without another thought, named him, "Shep."

Shep was instant entertainment, right out of the box. Until he arrived, our favorite activity had been pretending that the empty cologne bottles we rescued from the garbage were toy cars. We'd drive them all over the dirt pile in our side yard for hours. Shep made this activity that had once held our attention for hours seem downright dull.

Those bottles weren't even real toys, but Shep surely was a real dog. We taught him to speak, roll over, sit up, climb up to the first limb of a tree and even climb a stepladder. We propped a two by four up to a storage shed and he would follow us to the rooftop. Neighbors and visitors were amused to see Shep joining my brother and me when we played our souped-up version of king of the hill. We weren't supposed to be up there, but with Shep along, our petty crime was almost always forgotten.

Despite our excitement, Shep's arrival did cause one problem. The neighbors across the street, the Donovans, had a bulldog named "Chum." Nothing but the best for the Donovans, and Chum was a purebred. The Donovan farm was smaller than ours, but they had a nice home. They didn't have any cattle, or chickens or pigs, giving Chum the distinction of being the only animal on their farm. The Donovans weren't really farmers; they leased their land to other farmers on our road. Mr. Donovan worked as a foreman at a factory in Sparta and his wife, Marilyn was, as I overheard some of the neighbor men say, "a good looker." She worked as a secretary for the town's big shot, Paul Morley. He owned the only car dealership for miles, Morley Chevrolet.

Word among the area farmers was that Mr. Morley demanded a whole lot from his secretary, even some secret duties that we kids didn't understand at the time but that Mrs. Donovan was rumored to be willing to provide. We might not understand all the details, but we did see our pretty neighbor and her important boss pull into the Donovan's driveway in one of Mr. Morley's shiny new Chevy's, go into the house together, and then leave an hour later.

We weren't nosy, just observant. And besides, before my Ma bought us Shep, Gerald and I would walk across Squires Road to the Donovans to play with Chum. He was stocky and stoic and tolerated our attention even if he didn't actually invite it. Or so we thought.

Soon after Shep's arrival, Chum started coming to the edge of his yard to bark at us. It was as if he wasn't sure he wanted to play with him, but he was sure that he didn't want us playing with any other dog. Shep had been taught by my brothers and me to stay on our property, and I have to say that he did his best to ignore the canine insults coming from those slobbery jowls across the street.

Chum had his pride though, and didn't appreciate being snubbed. He'd edge closer and closer to our yard, sometimes planting himself squarely in the middle of the road like a fur-covered brick and barking.

I think my brothers and I knew that there was a limit to Shep's willingness to follow our commands where Chum was concerned. The day would come when he could no longer ignore the challenge of his only rival. When his doggie desires would overpower his attempts to "be a good boy." That day came in July.

The rest of our family was patriotic and we had treated Shep as one of us, so perhaps Shep was patriotic too, I don't know, but on the Fourth of July, he caused what can only be described as canine fireworks. My father had bought some sparklers for us kids and we were given two each.

Lavern chased Gerald and me with his sparklers and we all ran around in the front yard, with Shep joining in. He'd chase after a stick with a rag tied around the end of it, and then bring it back. The game we invented that day went like this: Lavern would toss the stick to the edge of the road where Shep would fetch it. Chum watched from his yard across the road, just like the kid who is always left out at recess. He barked his protest, over and over. A sound that we were so used to by now, we almost didn't hear it.

Then Chum barked louder, and then louder again, until there was a tone of desperation in his yelps. We could ignore him with our human ears, but Shep couldn't with his canine ones.

All of a sudden, Shep, who had totally ignored Chum for his entire young life, had heard all he could take without offering a response. Our happy-go-lucky shaggy dog walked slowly and determinedly to the edge of our property, looked at Chum, and gave him one singular angry bark. Just as if to say, "Look, I'm getting sick and tired of your yapping. If you want to mess with me, let's go."

Chum understood perfectly and didn't need a second invitation. He strutted across the road, growling all the way. The two sized each other up for just a brief second, then a wicked dogfight ensued. Instead of trying to break it up, we ran over to the fight like kids in a schoolyard and rooted loudly for Shep. We hooted as he dodged in and away from Chum, snapping at his legs. He was much quicker than the muscular Chum, who would whirl around to meet Shep face to face, but by then Shep would be out of his reach.

Soon though, the fight escalated and both dogs were locked together in combat, teeth to neck. That's when all the fun went out of it. This wasn't a game anymore. It turned serious. All three of us knew that this rivalry had turned frightening. Our two dogs were in a fight to the death. When it was over, one family on Squires Road wasn't going to have a pet anymore.

"Stop! Stop!" I heard a voice holler out.

I don't know how Ma got there so quick, or how she managed to bring along a pail of water with her. She moved right in on the death match and dumped the water, pail and all, on the two beasts, screaming as she did. It was a direct hit. No one was going to harm her magazine dog if she had anything to say about it.

I'm not sure if it was the icy well water or Ma's screaming, but the fight stopped and Chum ran for home, leaving a blood trail behind him. Shep stood in our yard facing his retreating foe, his head down, panting and bleeding.

Dad and Mrs. Donovan, both arrived minutes later, running in from opposite directions. Dad took one look at our now savage-looking Shep and at Ma's wet dress, and at the neighbor lady's panicked expression. "What to hell is going on?" he shouted, to no one in particular.

"I'm so sorry," Mrs. Donovan said. "I hope Chum didn't hurt your puppy."

Hurt our "puppy"? Was she crazy? Shep was no puppy, he was a superhero dog, our family security system, a prizefighter and a werewolf disguised as a family pet, all rolled into one. Standing off to the side, my brothers and I didn't dare challenge Mrs. Donovan in front of Dad, but we shook our heads and whispered under our breath to each other. "Shep was the winner. No way could Chum whip Shep. Good thing for Chum that Ma came out with the water."

If my Ma or Dad heard us, they didn't let on. Mrs. Donovan promised to keep Chum home and the incident was over—for a while.

Big Buster

All of our cows were white with black spots, a breed commonly known as Holsteins, the largest and most popular dairy cow in the U.S. Some of our neighbors had Jerseys or Guernsey's, which produced less milk, but with a higher butter fat content. Holstein milking cows are, on average, five foot high and weigh 1200 to 1400 pounds. They can be bred at thirteen to fifteen months, and will give birth about nine months later to an eighty to one hundred pound calf. They produce seven to ten times more milk than their calf needs, which is what makes them such a great dairy cow. The result is three to five gallons extra twice a day, every day. That's a lot of milk – more than a thousand quarts a month. And, believe it or not they were possessive of it.

Young cows being milked for the first time will kick the person trying to take their milk. Devices called kickers, which are similar to handcuffs, usually have to be added to a cow's ankles for their first milking. After about a week, most cows will give up and can be milked without kickers. My dad often sustained hand injuries trying to break in a young cow without kickers. After a week of hand milking, a milking machine was used. These machines had four suction cups which were attached to the cow to extract the milk.

Hand milking required technique and strong hands. My brothers and I, as well as other farmers, were amazed at how fast our dad could milk a cow. He worked his hands in a squeezing rhythm causing the milk to flow like a faucet.

The 6 a.m. and 6 p.m. milkings were placed in milk cans. The cans were in turn placed in a cooled water tank where they were later removed and shipped off to the diary. My dad always enjoyed and respected achievement. That's probably why he admired Bert. A young guy whose size had nothing to do with his age was our milkman. Bert towered over us at six feet and then some and well over 200 pounds, he was all muscle and speed. Dad would watch with admiration, as Bert would handle those 100-pound cans, one in each hand, and toss them into his refrigerated truck.

"Wouldn't want to mess with that boy," Dad would say. Bert hauled our milk to the dairy where it was pasteurized, bottled in quarts jars, and sold. Once a day, a quart or two of the fresh milk was poured into a pitcher for us. We drank non-pasteurized milk, straight from the cow to the kitchen and thought nothing of it. In fact, we often walked up to a cow, bent down, and squirted milk directly into our mouths. All dairy farmers did it back then. I wouldn't think of drinking non-pasteurized milk today, but I don't know of anyone that ever got sick from it.

Today, a lot of things about the dairy business are different. For one, cows are artificially bred from the sperm of a bull of proven bloodlines. In our day, each cow had to be bred the old fashioned way, by a bull owned by a farmer who provided stud service. Most farmers didn't want the headache of dealing with the cost and concerns of containing and feeding a bull – they were dangerous animals and downright mean. That's where stud service came in. The farmers who didn't own a bull themselves had to either haul their cows to a farm that did have one, or arrange with a farmer to bring the bull to them. Both these methods cost money, something we had little of.

Late one summer Saturday afternoon Dad came home from a farm auction, followed by a truck pulling a fifteen-foot long box stall trailer. Inside was a pure-bred Holstein bull. As the truck headed toward the barnyard, Gerald and I ran toward the truck, anxious to find out what could be inside. It was something huge, we could tell that much by the dark shape moving around inside.

"A bull!" Gerald yelled.

The powerfully built animal was bellowing out loud scary noises from inside his mobile stall. He was wearing a halter and two ropes were tied to it at one end, and tied to the stall walls at the other. His legs were each wrapped at the ankles with a rope, and those were tied to the side of the stall, too.

It took five full-grown men to get that bull out of the trailer. The truck driver, his helper, my dad, and two of our neighbors, Bob Donovan and Ray May, all worked together to guide the angry beast out of the trailer and into our yard, where they tied him to the trunk of an oak tree inside our fenced pasture. He stayed there for three days while my dad, Mr. Donovan, and Mr. May built a box stall just for him inside our barn. The project began the next morning with a lumberyard delivery of six by six square posts and boards that were five inches wide and two and a half inches thick.

The lumber truck elicited the same reaction from Gerald and me as the livestock trailer had. "Wow!" we said at the same time. We had never seen a bull that big, and we had never seen such big pieces of lumber, either.

Up early Sunday morning, Gerald and I headed for the barnyard, even before eating breakfast. Dad was already up and we found him in the barn, sledgehammer in hand, whacking away at the concrete floor where he intended to set those big posts in fresh cement.

Gerald and I cautiously climbed over the fence and walked closer to the big animal. Finally tired out from his day of struggling, the bull had lain down next to the oak tree he was still tied to. He was mostly black with various sized white spots. As we approached, he jumped to his feet, pulling his massive frame up with a quickness that contrasted with the slow movement we were used to seeing with the cows.

We took a big step back. We had heard enough about the behavior of bulls, and even seen some of it ourselves, to know enough to stay our distance. The night before, lying in our beds, we had both worried that our favorite climbing tree might be in danger. What if the bull pulled it down? Looking at it now, even with the bull's massive size and evil glint in his eyes, we could see that the oak was solidly grounded, with a diameter at its base over two feet wide.

My brother's reaction to all this was to give the monster a name "We will call him Big Buster," he decided.

As usual, I agreed with my brother. Several inches taller than me by this time, Gerald was calling most of the shots in our relationship. Back at the barn, Mr. Donovan and Mr. May came over to help my dad get started building the stall. Gerald and I watched and fetched tools, and then at dinner time we all called it a day. Everyone except Dad.

"Take a break Howard. You're going to wear yourself out," Mr. Donovan said as he was leaving for home.

"Just doing a little bit more, " Dad answered. Then, he proceeded to work into the night.

When Donovan and May came back the next day, they were amazed at how much my dad had done. Two days later Big Buster was moved into his new home. Good thing the stall was well built.

Big Buster initiated his new digs by ramming his head, powered by his 1200-pound body, into the sides of the walls.

My dad was a wise man in every aspect of the farm, but he wasn't perfect. On occasion he had to learn from a costly mistake. His first experience at using Big Buster was a disaster. The idea seemed logical enough; Buster needed a mate. My dad moved a young heifer that he thought was in heat into the pen with Big Buster for the night.

"Oh my God, oh my God!" my dad yelled out as all of us went to check on Big Buster the next morning. It was the first time I can remember him being upset enough to shed tears. The young heifer lay in a heap in the corner, blood scattered about the stall. The cow was long dead and yet Big Buster was still ramming his bloody head into her lifeless body. Apparently, the heifer chose not to cooperate with Big Buster's desires.

Dad put that first terrible experience behind him and learned how to deal with Big Buster. Supervision was required. He would lead the bull to a cow in the yard, rope on the harness in one hand and a sharp pitchfork in the other. A bull is generally fearless and accustomed to being in control of his surroundings. Big Buster had one exception; he quickly learned to be fearful of my dad's pitchfork. A few sharp jabs, strong enough to draw blood, quickly established who was boss.

I think those first few bloody jabs had some special meaning for my dad, a little payback for destroying that heifer. The big fella quickly decided that he preferred the pleasure of taking care of business with those heifers rather than messing with that pitchfork. After that first enlightening experience with the fork, Dad only had to wave it in the air to get Big Buster to obey.

Paul the Auctioneer

Later that summer I heard the story of how Dad happened to buy Big Buster. While making an egg delivery to the Donovans, I heard Bob Donovan telling his brother how he had attended an auction with my dad. Seems they were about to leave, not having found any good deals, when the auctioneer said something that kept them there a few minutes longer.

"Hold up folks. The prize of this auction is about to be brought out," he said. His name was Paul Morley and he was known for miles as a man who could sell corn to a crow. He would stand up on a crate and tip his head back and let his bold voice announce one item after another. He could make anything sound like a deal. On that day he was up there on his crate, looking out over an audience of about fifty farmers gathered around a roped off circle where the cows and young heifers had just all been auctioned off.

"You're about to see the best Holstein bull in Muskegon County. This big fella will breed your whole herd and your neighbors' herd, too."

Morley, always neatly dressed in denim slacks and a blue short sleeve shirt with a Morley Chevrolet logo on it, was a small but nice looking man, with light brown hair on a well-built frame. In addition to owning the Ravenna Chevrolet dealership, Morley was an auctioneer and often bought farms that were in financial difficulty. Soon after buying a farm, he would conduct an auction on the livestock and machinery, often raising enough money to cover most of his purchase. He would then sell the land and buildings for a profit.

The bull was brought out to the edge of the circle by five men, tied up much like Gerald and I had seen later, when he was delivered to our farm. The bull was pawing, moaning and snorting, and the crowd took a collective step back.

"OK folks," Morley said. "We're gonna start out low. One thousand dollars. Too low a price for this fine bull."

In rapid succession, with the words running together in a musical tone, Morley yelled out, "Anybody buy, anybody buy, anybody buy, anybody buy." He rattled off the words loudly and so fast you could hardly understand them, though this was his signature line and everybody knew what they were. Even so, no one bid.

"All right, let's get this started. How about the ridiculous price of eight hundred dollars?" Then, more yelling out of, "Anybody buys." Still no response.

After several attempts, and working his way down to six hundred dollars, Morley looked at one of the farmers and said, "Come on John, this is steal at this price." And he might have sold him for that, too but the bull went into a rage, jerking one of the rope holders to the ground. Another man had to come to the first man's rescue and the bull was finally contained.

"Wouldn't take that beast if you paid me the $600," said farmer John.

"Ok, ok someone give me an offer." A long pause ensued.

"Fifty bucks," my dad barked out. Morley laughed and others joined in.

"And that has to include hauling that bugger to my farm and tying him to my oak tree," my dad added.

Morley laughed. " Ok, Howard Lobdell has put in a bid of fifty dollars. Who wants to go five hundred? How about four, or three? We can't sell this bull for fifty dollars." Still, no other takers.

"Ok boys, fifty dollars going once, and fifty dollars going twice, fifty dollars going three times. Sold for $50 to Howard Lobdell."

Dad was happy for the bargain and confident that he could find a way to tame that bull. He also thought about how he would be saving several hundred dollars a year in stud fees and how he could have that bull paid for in a couple months with stud fees from neighboring farmers.

His math would have been good if it hadn't been for that young heifer. She was worth two hundred dollars, at least, maybe more.

Dad's Roots

My dad's desire to return to the farm seemed to be in his blood. He was born in a log cabin in 1909, four days before William Howard Taft took office as President. His father, Edward Lobdell, was born in 1875, while Ulysses S. Grant was President. Edward had built his log cabin on a forty- acre plot where he and his wife, Martha Peterson Lobdell raised three sons and two daughters.

The Lobdell family lived off small crops of fruits and vegetables, supplemented by Grandpa Lobdell's part-time income from logging jobs. Edward's father, Chester, born in 1847 (James Polk was the President then), and grandfather, James, born in 1818 (James Monroe) were also loggers and farmers. James, my great, great grandfather, was the first Sheriff of Michigan's Muskegon County in 1859. James also served as an officer in a very special Civil War cavalry, The Michigan 6th Cavalry in 1862 and 1863. My favorite uncle, the one I remember most, was Uncle 'Alf' Alfred. He was my Dad's older brother, and was known for not liking to work. He was about six feet tall and weighed about 130 pounds, ate very little, and smoked a lot of Phillip Morris cigarettes. Alf's diet consisted of coffee, Ludens cough drops, soup, a slice of bread, and more Phillip Morris cigarettes. This was what he put in his mouth, for breakfast, lunch and dinner.

Not surprisingly, Uncle Alf never married, and lived at home with Grandpa Ed and Grandma Martha for most of his life. In a matter of weeks after Grandpa DeWilder passed away, along came Uncle Alf to live with us on the farm. Grandpa Ed, had died of a stroke in 1942, leaving Uncle Alf alone with his mother, Grandma Martha, who had gone blind. Alf wasn't of much help to her, so Grandma eventually moved in with her daughter, Hazel, and Uncle Alf moved in with us.

Uncle Alf always had "pain." We never knew where the pain was or what caused it, but whenever my Dad asked him if he could help with some chores, the pain suddenly got worse. For a guy known to be tough, my Dad sure was a sucker for people in need. The one thing I remember about Uncle Alf is that he favored me in anything that happened around the house. On the rare occasion that we had a dessert, Uncle Alf would give his share to me.

"That little guy is gonna be a winner someday," he would say, to no one in particular.

1910. Howard in lower left, held by mother;. Father, Ed; grandfather, Chester; and grandmother Mary, sitting with brothers and sister.

Bessie Must Have Her Way

Milking cows spend much of their life in stalls with a metal stanchion around their neck. The stanchion keeps them in place for milking and feeding. They stand in those stalls all winter long. They sleep there, are fed there, and are milked there. The body heat of a herd of cows is a powerful force, and dairy barns never need heat, even on the coldest winter days, even in northern Michigan.

My brothers and I didn't much like chores, but they became routine for us and we did them without complaint. Still, we all agreed on what was our least favorite one. That was cleaning the gutters – the troughs constructed just behind the cows to catch their manure while they're locked in, standing in their stalls.

Even though we kept our barn pretty clean, our cousins from the city plugged their noses whenever they came for a visit and walked into our barn. With twenty-five to thirty-five head of cattle in a barn, the smell of cow manure can overpower a first time visitor. At any given time, somewhere down the line of cows, one of them is making a deposit into the gutter. First time visitors always grimaced with embarrassment at the sight. Farm kids thought nothing of it. My parents, my brothers, and I became so accustomed to the conditions in the barn that we were only subconsciously aware. We would, however, get a good chuckle at the reactions of our city relatives.

Once a day my father, or one of us boys when we got old enough, would drive the tractor pulling the manure spreader through the barn so the manure could be shoveled into the spreader and taken to the field for fertilizer. In winter, we'd use a wheelbarrow to haul the manure to the barnyard where it aged until spring, when we could spread it in the fields. I always thought it was amusing that what disgusted my cousins in the winter, was the same substance that made them rave over our sweet corn, and strawberries, and tomatoes, in the summer.

Today, my grandchildren giggle at the idea of all that cow manure. Their favorite story from my childhood is about one of our cows, Bessie. Every farm that has dairy cows has at least one member of the herd named Bessie, and she's usually a favorite. It's an unspoken farm tradition, I think. My grandchildren love to hear about Bessie's favorite stall. Here's the story I tell them:

In the summer the cows are very happy to be able to leave the barn after milking and feed in the pasture. I think they may even remember how long and dull winters are while they're grazing with their heads down and the sun shining on their backs. The first day in the spring, when they get to leave their stalls after being cooped up for five smelly months, is truly a special occasion. As kids, we loved to watch this annual event. The cows kicked up their heels just like in the nursery rhyme, and we almost believed they could take flight and really jump over the moon.

As each spring day neared evening milking time, with Shep's help my brothers and I would herd the cows back to the barn. When they walked inside single file, they'd usually just walk into the first open stall. Cows are fed grain in the barn, and to them it's like dessert after a dinner of grass, so they're usually anxious to get inside a stall. Any stall.

For some unknown reason of bovine wisdom, our favorite cow had a favorite stall. Bessie had to have the second stall. The first, third, or any other stall just would not do. When another cow got to her stall first, Bessie would just stand there in front of her favorite stall and beller. Loud. The line of cows would stop and milking would be delayed, if only for a few minutes. Dad had no patience for such shenanigans though, and would force poor Bessie to go into the next open stall. On these days Dad would invariably complain at dinner about our favorite cow.

"I just can't understand why Bessie didn't give very much milk today."

I understood. "You gotta let Bessie have her favorite stall," I'd tell him.

"Aw, poppycats," my dad would say. "The stall don't give the milk, the cow does."

After weeks of sporadic output by Bessie, one day my dad decided to test my theory. "Ok Wayne," he said, "your job today is to see to it that Bessie gets in the second stall."

I took charge of my new duty with all the seriousness with which it was given, and Bessie trotted happily into her second stall. There was no holdup in the single file of cows that day, no bellering, and no lack of milk.

"By golly, I can't believe it, but you were right, son," Dad said as he came inside for dinner after the evening milking. "That darn cow gave more milk from that second stall." I was pleased and didn't even mind that I'd inherited another regular evening chore.

Secrets with Ronald

1950 was the year Harry Truman faced the power of the hydrogen bomb, Shirley Temple retired from show business, Dizzy Trout pitched for the Detroit Tigers, and potatoes came to Hoogstraat schoolhouse. I was nine years old that year, in the fifth grade, and all I could think about was how badly I wanted a new Superman lunch box. Instead, I got a potato. Gerald and I both did.

Earlier that fall the school board got it into their heads that our little one-room schoolhouse needed a kitchen, and so they voted in favor of spending the money to add one. The school would pay for the lumber and nails and shingles and a crew of men from our town, mostly fathers of students at the school, would volunteer to build it.

And build it they did. The kitchen was small, but it had a stove and a sink and a counter and cupboards. The building crew, which included my dad, some other fathers and even Wally Wagoner, the snobbish farmer we were in awe of because his vegetables were always so perfect looking at the farm market. The kitchen went together lickety-split, and was operational after just a week of evenings and weekends of volunteer labor.

Such an accomplishment was newsworthy in our little town, and as soon as the project was finished we were all told that a reporter from our local newspaper, the Ravenna Times, would be coming by the next afternoon to take a picture of the proud building crew. Getting your picture in the paper was the great equalizer – every man, rich or poor, farmer or laborer, wanted to stand up and be counted right there in black and white. To a man, the dads all arranged to be there, even though some of them must have had to take time off work to do it.

At the specified time, the men gathered in the kitchen, waiting for the reporter to arrive with his camera and notebook. All at once, the door to the schoolhouse opened and in walked Wally Wagoner. He didn't look like a farmer though; he was wearing a suit and tie for the big occasion. The kids snickered into their hands and couldn't look Mr. Wagoner in the eye, but the men weren't that polite. They laughed right out loud.

"Hey there Wally, looks like your wife dressed ya!" someone said.

Wally stood as still as our flag post and his face turned the color of the red stripes that hung there. He balled his hands up into fists, pressed his lips together and ran back out the door. When the Ravenna Times published the picture of the smiling work crew, each man clad in their well-worn overalls, Wally was nowhere to be seen.

The new kitchen was the talk of the town for a week after that photograph appeared. It would be used mainly for school events but Mrs. Lindgren was allowed "limited use" of the stove at lunchtime. That's where the potatoes came in. "Limited use" was just that – the stove could only be used for one thing: heating up the whole, unpeeled potatoes her students brought from home.

In the morning after we said the Pledge of Allegiance, Mrs. Lindgren would open the stove, set the dial to "warm" and line up our potatoes on the top rack. They were cooked through by lunchtime. This was a good development for Gerald and me because we grew potatoes on the farm and always had an ample supply. I might not have had a superhero lunch box, but I had a potato every day to go along with my peanut butter and jelly sandwich. Some kids only had the sandwich. I was still envious of the few kids who did have a metal lunch boxes, sometimes even with a store-bought cookie inside, but a potato was at least something.

My favorite day of every school year was the last one. Or, rather, the day before summer vacation. We spent a half day getting our report cards, playing outside, having a picnic, and then were set free to run home for the whole, long summer.

The summer of 1950 was a year of great progress for the Lobdell family. We finally got a telephone. We might have been the last family in our area to join the party line phone system, but when it finally came our ring worked just as good as anyone else's.

Our line's ring was three long and two short. Since we were on a party line shared by a number of families, the phone would ring on and off throughout the day and evening, but we were only supposed to answer it when we heard our special ring.

That little telephone of ours sat on a shelf in the corner, and I imagined it hearing all sorts of things that weren't meant for our ears. Of course, if you wanted to be a "Nosy Rosie" you could sneak a listen to another person's call. I would sometimes snoop on my friend Ronald, but the voice I was aching to hear was Jacqueline's.

With her smooth ponytail and white teeth, I thought Jacqueline was the prettiest girl at Hoogstraat school, maybe even the prettiest girl in America. And I wasn't the only one who thought so. Everybody else loved Jacqueline too, including our usually stern teacher. Sometimes she would actually smile at Jacqueline.

Given her special status, I felt inadequate to be Jacqueline's friend, even though she was always polite and smiled at me. I looked forward to seeing her at school, enjoyed her occasional smile at me and, of course, talked about her with Ronald. Still, I couldn't eavesdrop on her with our telephone even if I dared to because her family was on a different party line.

Besides the phone, our family marked other progress that year, too. My dad, now making good headway with the farm, traded in his used Farmall tractor for a new one. He also traded in his seventeen-year-old 1933 rusted out Chevy. The kids on our road made that Chevy the butt of a lot of jokes, so we weren't sad to see that heap leave the farm. Between the time Dad announced we'd be getting a new car and drove away in that old junker and before he came back home, Gerald and I fantasized about what he'd bring back. A sports car maybe, or a shiny red pickup truck. I bragged to my friend Ronald that our family was getting a new car.

After school, Gerald and I raced home, even though Dad wouldn't be home for hours. We waited in the front yard, sitting in the grass doing nothing but watching every vehicle that came down Squires Road. When our new car drove toward the house, we didn't even notice it at first. When we saw Dad behind the wheel, Gerald and I couldn't quite believe what he was coming home with. There he was, grinning from ear to ear, both hands on the steering wheel of a 1934 two door Chevy. Of course the car was in excellent condition, but other than that, it looked just exactly like the 1933 he'd left with that morning. Our "new" car was even the same dull black color.

Now that my brothers and I were out of school, we were expected to do more work on the farm but we also had more time to play with Shep. He was an amazing dog, and tried his darnedest to do everything we asked. He rolled over, sat up, barked on command and would actually climb a ladder. Gerald and I would set up a ladder and say,

"Come on Shep, up, up, up," and he would climb that ladder, paw by paw. He was hesitant and became frustrated at the top trying to turn to go back down, usually just jumping, but that dog wouldn't refuse to try anything we asked.

Wandering was his only bad habit. He would take off in the evenings, roaming the countryside after dark. I'm not sure where he went or what he did, but he would disappear every night at dark, with one exception. If our parents left for the evening, Shep would sit on the porch and not leave until our parents came home. He must have decided that we needed protection. Shep was smart and considerate. Qualities rarely found together in a person, let alone a dog.

Another Challenge

Besides being the year we got a telephone, 1950 was also the year of the grudge match between Shep and Chum. Chum had remained quiet for a whole year. The first scrap between the two of them had halted his barking, but not for good, unfortunately.

Maybe bulldogs have short memories, but for some reason Chum started coming to the edge of his property again that summer, watching our comings and goings and keeping busy with his yapping.

The first time it happened, Shep took a few steps toward the road, looked at the barking bulldog and turned around and walked back, as if to say, " Hey Chum, get a life." Chum was as persistent as he was irritating though. He never let up. It was almost as if he were waiting for a challenge.

That challenge came again on the 4th of July. Same dogs, same routine. Chum barked and Shep had enough. He calmly walked to the edge of our property and barked back at Chum, as if to say, "Ok Chum, you want to give it another try?"

And Chum was up for it. He dashed across the road into our yard to a ready and waiting Shep. The dogs were yapping, growling, and biting each other. They were out to kill. Once again, my mother came running and screaming with the pail of water. The injuries were even more severe than the first time the two dogs had fought. Chum had to be taken to the vet and Shep suffered some wounds on his face. My father and Mrs. Donovan engaged in a heated discussion, ending in Mrs. Donovan agreeing to keep Chum home.

She did – for another year.

Trains and Bikes

Being the last kids in the neighborhood to get everything was tough, especially when what everyone else had was a bicycle. I can't count the number of times Gerald and I sat on our porch talking about how much fun it would be to have a bike, imagining all the places we could go.

To make our longing for two-wheeled freedom worse, we watched other kids ride by our house on their bikes, the fun they were having plainly showing on their faces. For months leading up to Christmas that year, Gerald and I asked our parents for bikes. There had been progress at school, progress on the farm, and my Dad even had a new car – well, new to him anyway. We were hoping there'd be progress under the Christmas tree, too.

On Christmas Eve, our family's traditional day for opening presents, Dad sat us down in the front room to give us the bad news.

"We can't afford bikes this year," he said. "If we have a good year on the farm next year, we will get you bikes. But we did get you an electric train set to share." He paused to see our disappointed reaction, and then added, "We want you to go to the wash room and wait while we set the train set up."

Gerald and I hung our heads and wandered silently through the kitchen and into the washroom. We were farm kids, Lobdells, experienced at surviving disappointment. The thought of a train set began to have some appeal. Maybe there would be real smoke puffing from the engine, I said to Gerald.

When we opened the door to the washroom though, there sat two bikes. They were not new bikes, but they were good bikes. We were thrilled and taught ourselves to ride on a bright snowy day after Christmas. I can still feel how those bike tires slipped and slid in the snow, sending a spray of white up behind us as we rode.

My father liked playing little tricks and teasing us, and I think his grin watching us ride those bikes in the snow was as big as mine and Gerald's combined. We may have been the last to get goodies, but we sure relished them when they finally came.

Trouble in '51

For Ravenna farm kids like us, there was someone worse out there than our schoolteacher, Garnet Lindgren; we just didn't know it yet. We were however, about to find out real soon. The day after Labor Day in 1950, our rag-tag group assembled at the doors of Hoogstraat, gritting our teeth against the injustice and imprisonment of another school year.

Summer vacation was over, our freedom was going to be held hostage in this one room schoolhouse for the next nine months, and we all just had to face it. Instead of holding Fourth of July sparklers, we'd better get used to holding pencils.

No more running through the woodlot on an adventure; we had to quit wiggling and sit still in our seats. By the fifth grade I should have been used to the way that the start of school yanked you by your overall straps right out of summer, but the first day of school vexed me just the same. I could have prepared for that if I thought about it long enough, but what I had no way of preparing for was the new teacher.

Once we were all inside and seated, a big and old woman with a sour look on her face waddled to the front of the room and looked around at the crowd of skinny kids in worn clothes sitting in front of her. She introduced herself as our new teacher, adding that Mrs. Lindgren had taken a year off from teaching us our lessons for "personal medical reasons."

I couldn't imagine what a "personal medical reason" was. Weren't all medical-type things personal? When Ma had a baby, that was personal. When Lavern cracked his head open, that was personal. Maybe Mrs. Lindgren was going to have a baby. Or, maybe she cracked her head open. It seemed like if either one of these things were the reason that she wasn't coming back to school, we would have already heard about it. Over the party line maybe or from all the moms talking to each other. But we hadn't, and so her personal reason remained a mystery.

Mrs. Bennett, however, was all too clear. No mystery there, she was one poor excuse for a teacher. It wasn't that she was big or old, though she was both of these things. It was more that she was, plain and simple, unhappy. Miserable even. And, she took an immediate dislike first to Ronald and then to me. I still can't understand why.

Later, she would have had good reason, with all the paper spit wads we threw and the school days we skipped. But she took a dislike to us right away, before she even had the chance to get to know us.

As for the schoolwork she came up with, it was boring. Or, maybe it was boring because she assigned it to us in her boring voice. The work wasn't difficult exactly; I just didn't feel like doing it. Once, I lost a list of spelling words on my way home from school. There was going to be a spelling test the next afternoon, and I had planned to memorize the words at home that night. When I got home though, the list wasn't in my school bag and it wasn't in any of my pockets. I didn't worry too much about it; I'd just get to school early tomorrow and get another copy of the list and study a little before the other kids got there.

When the next day came, I got to Hoogstraat ten minutes early, walked up to Mrs. Bennett's desk and asked her if she would give me another list of the words to study.

"Too late now," she said, her fleshy face warping into a sarcastic grin. She pounded her elbows down on her desk for emphasis and I jumped. She held my gaze and dared me to defy her. At issue was just a list of spelling words but we both knew it was about a lot more than that. It was strange being in the classroom alone with her, without any of the other kids. During the school day I hated her; now, she was scary.

"The test will be given at 9 a.m.," she said.

"Why 9?" I asked. Up until this moment, we always had our spelling tests right after lunch.

"You don't question me, young man. I'm the teacher. You are the student."

She spit out the word "student" as if it were an insult. I ran away from her desk and could almost feel her rabid grin follow me out the door. I raced down the path that led away from the schoolyard and met up with Ronald, on his way in. I took a quick look at Ronald's copy of the list; not too bad, mostly just states and Presidents. Mrs. Bennett didn't have much imagination. She could have slipped in something interesting like "inaugurate" or "presidential" but she never did.

That week I misspelled one word, "Rosevelt" instead of "Roosevelt." Score one for me. But another time Mrs. Bennett gave me "an important math test" the morning after I had been out sick for two days. I flunked that one. Score one for Mrs. Bennett. Near the end of the school year though, another "important math test" was given. I was only one of three in the class to score one hundred percent. Mrs. Bennett – one, Wayne – two.

Even though I kept score, it was obvious to me and to everyone else that I wasn't the only kid in school she had it in for. Mrs. Bennett used the same mean tactics on Ronald.

I didn't like my teacher and had no intention of trying to win her over. The feelings were mutual, and I knew that there was no way I was going to please her, even if I did decide to try. The spit wads and the skipped days of school and coming in late from recess day after day was our way, Ronald's and mine, to rebel against her tactics. I didn't even have to say a word, and just let my actions speak for themselves.

For her part, Mrs. Bennett had a way to get even with Ronald and me, too. Report cards. And she didn't have to say anything, either. When the report cards came out at the end of the year, mine read, "Repeat fifth grade." Ronald got the same message on his card: "Repeat sixth grade."

Mrs. Bennett might not have been a very good teacher, but she was a smart one. She knew the number one rule of discipline back in those days: Parents would back up the wrath of schoolteachers with wrath of their own at home. Today's teachers can never be sure whether the notes and report cards that go home will even be read, but back then that wasn't the case. True to their generation, Ma and Dad were horrified.

"We hoped you were the smart one!" they chided, when they opened up my report card. Later, they tried to get my teacher to change her mind but Mrs. Bennett's word was law in that school, and nothing I or my parents said or thought would change anything. I would have to repeat fifth grade, just like the card said.

In later years, Ma took to explaining how I came to be a year older than any of my classmates by saying that I started school when I was six instead of five. I've carried that lie with me all my life until now.

What seems like punishment at the time can sometimes turn out to be providence. When I think back now, I thank God that I had Mrs. Bennett for a teacher, and that she despised me enough to hold me back from the next grade. Had I been progressed to sixth grade on schedule, I would have ended up at Ravenna High School instead of Muskegon High School, and my life would have been on an entirely different path. I likely would not have met the single most important person in my life.

In March of 1951, Lavern quit school. Not because he couldn't do the schoolwork, he just couldn't stay out of trouble. If you think I crossed horns with Mrs. Bennett, you should have seen how Lavern interacted with his teachers at Ravenna High School. First, he was expelled for setting off a stink bomb in a hallway. Then, he got caught drinking hard cider on school grounds. When word came back to Hoogstraat that Lavern had quit high school, Mrs. Lindgren crowed out the news to the whole class.

"I knew that would happen," she said. "He's nothing but a bum and always will be."

Gerald and I slouched down in our seats.

Two weeks later, Lavern left home one day to answer a help wanted advertisement for selling magazines. He didn't come home.

City Cousins

Our cousins from the city loved to come to the farm to visit us, especially cousin David, who was my age, and cousin Leo, who was Gerald's. They were brothers too, my mother's sister Grace's two sons. In the summer of 1951 they were with us for two weeks. They arrived on a day we planned to go to one of Paul Morley's auctions.

My dad went to these auctions often. They provided a chance to buy some used equipment or cows at a good price. The sad part about them was that they usually took place because someone was losing their farm due to foreclosure. Our cousins found Mr. Morley's rapid-fire yelling to be amusing. Leo and David were actually half brothers. Aunt Grace Benton had previously married a man by the name of Leo Watkins. Leo Sr. was a temperamental and even a somewhat dangerous man.

While we were still living in Muskegon, Watkins came at Aunt Grace with a gun. My dad took the gun away from Leo and wrestled him to the floor. A few years later, after divorcing Aunt Grace, Leo Watkins Sr. shot his new wife and himself, a traumatic event for my cousins. Consequently, Leo Jr. was rebellious, and often got into fist fights with other boys, including my brother Gerald. The relatives thought a few weeks on the farm might do him some good. Well, yes and no.

"Stop or I'll Shoot!"

One evening in August, just after dark, the four of us boys were standing out in the yard together as boys do, kicking at the dirt and listening to the crickets get going. For no particular reason, Gerald said he had a hankering for apples.

It would have been easy enough for our cousins and Gerald and me to just snack on apples from our own skimpy little trees. After all, to boys our age an apple is pretty much an apple. But Gerald had to go on and bring up Red Delicious, how sweet they were, how juicy, and so of course then nothing else would satisfy us that night. Gerald made them sound as good as apple pie, and made us feel like it was our God-given right to have some. Right then, too.

As far as we knew, there was only one place to get apples like the ones Gerald described: Wally Wagoner's place. Far away apples always seemed to taste sweeter than apples in our own yard and so our cousins David and Leo, and my brother Gerald and I, headed out on the mile and a half-long hike across our own property and the two other farms that stood between us and Mr. Wagoner's now legendary apple orchard.

Wally Wagoner knew apples and he grew prizewinners every summer. Gerald and I had seen them many times stacked and washed and waxed and shined at the farmer's market. They were big as baseballs and just as solid too, holding their juicy white flesh inside tight blood-red skins. When you bit into one, it tasted like every sweet day of the whole sunny summer.

As we tiptoed into Mr. Wagoner's orchard that evening though, our hearts sank: his trees had already been picked clean. There was such a word-of-mouth demand for Wagoner apples that it was actually news in the neighborhood when they were finally ripe. And as soon as they were ripe, they were picked. A few shriveled specimens could be seen way up in the tops of a couple of the trees, but those were not what we had come all this way for, not even close. And so the four of us ran through the dark orchard, checking each row just to be sure, but the trees were all the same. Bare.

Gerald and I didn't want to admit it, but we were sure that we were too late. Our poor cousins, they had never even tasted Wagoner Delicious and now they never would. At least not for another year. Until, that is, we looked toward Mr. Wagoner's house. There in his front yard was a perfectly shaped apple tree loaded with apples so big, they looked to us at that distance just like red watermelons.

There was only one problem: that tree was so close to his house, Mr. Wagoner could probably keep a close eye on it from his bedroom window. As a matter of fact, that tree was probably his family's personal apple stash. The other trees in the orchard provided apples for market, but not this one. This one fed his family, no doubt about it.

That fact alone should have been enough to protect that tree from the likes of us, but it didn't. Under the direction of Gerald and Leo, we all decided to belly-crawl the last hundred feet to reach the tree. We were army soldiers, the tree was now the war zone, and if we had anything to say about it, our quarry would be had. The plan worked just fine and before we knew it, we were resting under that tree, looking up at the fruit hanging low in the branches, just asking to be picked.

"What about their dog?" I whispered.

"Shhh! They probably keep the dog in the house," Gerald assured us.

As it happened, he was right. The dog was not a problem. The problem was that we had to stand up in order to pick the apples. And once we saw them, any thought we once had of stealth or security or sneakiness bounced right out of our heads.

Gerald and Leo were older than David and me, and taller too. We both knew we were on our own for supply. No way would Gerald and Leo share, or lend one finger to help us. We had to jump to reach those beauties, and jump we did. There we were, all doing a shake down on Wally Wagoner's personal apple tree, completely unaware of how conspicuous we were to the occupants inside the house.

First we heard the back door open, and then we saw Wally Wagoner rushing outside, straight for us.

Leo found his voice first. "Hit it!" he yelled.

We all tore headlong for the safety of the dark orchard. I was first out, Gerald and Leo were right behind me, then came David, struggling to hang onto his apples while he ran.

"Stop or I'll shoot!" yelled Mr. Wagoner.

What kind of threat was that? No way was Mr. Wagoner going to shoot us. Your apples or your life? It was even kinda funny when you thought about it, and we all started laughing while we ran. All of us, that is, except David. Where was that cousin, anyway? I kept pumping my arms and running, keeping up with Gerald and Leo, sneaking a look behind me while I ran. David. He had hit the deck. It looked like at least one of us took the threat of bullets for apples seriously.

"That stupid little shit!" growled Leo, "Now we're all gonna git it!"

We all threw ourselves down on the ground in a line on our bellies and watched through the growing darkness as Mr. Wagoner grabbed David by the arm and yanked him back toward his house and his special tree and the scene of the crime. When they both disappeared inside, the three of us took off in the opposite direction.

We talked about the trouble we'd be in, but there wasn't anything else to do but run for home. When we got back to our farm, Mr. Wagoner's car was parked in our driveway. He had delivered David to the lion's den and the rest of us were going to have to face Dad, too. Of course, David had 'fessed up, and gave his confession first to Mr. Wagoner and then again to Dad. We all got a lecture and were told in no uncertain terms to give back our apple loot to Mr. Wagoner.

The next day, I watched Gerald and Leo sitting on our porch together, each with a Red Delicious apple in their hands, grins on their faces and juice running down their chins. Dad came by and I cringed to think what he was going to do to them when he saw how guilty they both still were. He raised an eyebrow, shook his head and grinned. I was empty-handed after our little adventure, but David wasn't. He didn't have one of Wally Wagoner's apples to show for it, but he did have something that lasted a lot longer. A new nickname. For the next week whenever Gerald or Leo would see him they'd yell, "Stop or I'll shoot!" Then they'd have a good laugh.

Patricia and the County Fair

Every day, Ma prayed for a letter from Lavern. A year passed though, without so much as one word from him. At first, Dad didn't act worried and he even told Ma to calm down. He said he had heard a rumor that Lavern had joined a band of traveling magazine salesmen and Dad thought the rumor could very well be true. His oldest son had simply gone to seek his fortune off the farm. The family would hear from Lavern soon, my dad was sure of it. After months and months went by though, even he put aside his cavalier attitude and started to worry. Dad hardly ever spoke of Lavern after that, and it got so that he hardly ever spoke about anything else, either. He carried his worry around in silence; Ma though, had other ways to handle what was knotting her up inside.

First, she turned detective. I don't know where she found it but my mother obtained a list of magazine sales companies and wrote letters to all of them, inquiring after the possibility that they may have hired a young man by the distinctive name of Lavern Lobdell. She didn't hear back from a single one of those companies. Not an answer to her letter, not a phone call, not even any scant details to add to the rumor that Lavern was seeing the country and knocking on doors out there, somewhere.

Ma went to sleep at night thinking about Lavern, and woke up thinking about him in the morning. In her waking hours, she tried to keep her worst fears in check. At night, that wasn't always possible, and sometimes Gerald and I could hear her crying, and calling out his name.

One day, Ma came up with another idea to help relieve some of her pain. She got herself a daughter. Well, a foster daughter, but my mother acted like she finally had the daughter she had always wanted, the daughter she hoped I would have been when she gave birth to me. That was when Patricia Smith, a fourteen-year-old ward of the state, came to live with us on the farm.

I can only imagine what Ma thought it would be like to finally have a daughter. She probably thought they would cook together, go on errands together, and pick out female type stuff like new curtains together. She'd finally have someone to show her catalog finds to, and to help her hem her dresses and hang out the washing. The only problem with Ma's fantasy was that Patricia preferred to spend her time with men and boys. To my mother's continual frustration, her "daughter" paid her no mind at all. Not only that, she didn't want to be called "Patricia" or even "Patty." She was just "Pat."

Pat was a diversion for my parents though. She was a troubled child from a troubled home and they were sure they could fix her up just fine with a good bath, a good meal, some hard work, and a little kindness. Ma, Dad, Uncle Alfred, our other relatives and even the neighbors thought Pat was just a wayward sweetheart. She was about 5'6", average build for a teenage girl, light brown hair, blue eyes and even pretty. For a tomboy, anyway. The grownups all thought Pat could do no wrong. Gerald and I knew better.

Pat would sneak Uncle Alfred's cigarettes, swear when adults were not around, and give my mother the finger the second she turned around. Proof, as far as I was concerned, that mothers do not have eyes in the backs of their heads. Where this ragamuffin girl was concerned, the grownups I had respected and even feared were suddenly blind as old dogs in the daylight.

I kept waiting for Pat to get what she had coming. I had a lot of waiting to do for that to happen, but there was at least one good thing that coincided with her coming to live with us; we finally were able to enter heifers in the Ravenna Fair.

"Shortest straw stays home with yer Mom." Holding three straws in his hand, Dad had us each draw one. He was on his way to buy some heifers and he had us draw straws to see who could go and who would have to stay home with my mother. We were getting bigger now, Gerald and I and now that we had Pat too, four in the cab of his Chevy pickup truck was too many.

I lost. Which, it turned out, was a much bigger defeat than just missing out on this trip and doing girly chores with Ma for the day. I held back my tears on that straw draw, but let them out full blast when the buying party returned with three heifers. Pat and Gerald had picked the biggest, healthiest-looking and prettiest heifers for themselves. A little scrawny one was left over for me.

I tried to take comfort in the fact that it was still only early June, giving the three of us two months to train our heifers for the August, 1952 Ravenna County Fair. I thought it was going to be fun, even with my sad excuse for a cow. I was wrong.

"Pat, boys, time to walk your heifers," Ma would yell out to us.

Two and three times a day we had to stop our fun to lead those stupid cows. We walked them in circles, training them to follow and stop with a jerk on the halter.

"Pat, boys, time to groom your heifers."

We hated to hear those words, but couldn't escape them, no matter where we were on the property. Mr. May, our neighbor a half-mile away, would later claim to have heard my mother's calls.

It did get better, though. I named my heifer Little Bessie, and my interest in her increased as the summer progressed. Little Bessie was filling out, shaping up well in fact. Plus, her white hair was beginning to shine. When the light was right, she shone even more than the other two.

"That one is not so little anymore," Dad said to me one day. "She is looking like a winner."

Once, I even saw Ma in the barn by herself, grooming Little Bessie. That's not anything the other female in our lives would ever do. For her part, my new "sister" always seemed to have money from her uncle to spend. Her game was to pay Gerald and me to groom her heifer.

After a summer's worth of work and waiting, the big day finally came. The Fair was held over one entire weekend and livestock couldn't be left at the fairgrounds alone so Gerald, Pat, and I had the dubious pleasure of caring for and staying with our heifers in the exhibition tent for two days—and that included sleeping next to them. We had to wait until Saturday afternoon for our competition. Little did we know that Ma, too had been planning to compete at the fair. And she got her chance to try her vocal skills first thing in the morning.

Among the Ravenna Fair activities in 1952 was a husband-calling contest. A microphone and loudspeakers were set up and about twenty wives lined up to take their turn. The object was to see who could yell their husband's name the loudest. The winner would get a fancy new cowbell. Three volunteer judges discussed how difficult it might be to select a winner. They didn't know my mother; she was fourth in line.

The first contestant let out with a little squeak for her husband, John. The second contestant was much louder and the third was another squeaker. Then came Ma. She took that microphone in her two hands and opened her mouth wide and let out with a "H O W A R D!" so loud that it scared the wits out of all downtown Ravenna. My brothers told me later that they heard her clearly all the way from the cow tent. Little Bessie, lying down at the time, must have thought Ma was coming to groom her cause my sweet heifer jumped to her feet at the ready.

Those other sixteen wives in line just turned and walked away. The announcer, jiggling his fingers in his ears, handed the cowbell to my Mom. The crowd was clapping their hands and cheering like crazy but I'm not sure many heard the noise they were making. Ma had yelled half of them temporarily deaf.

Saturday afternoon was the kids' turn for glory. That's when the judging of our heifers would take place and, best of all, some kids were going to get ribbons. Competition was fierce. More than fifty heifers were tied up to a wood fence in four rows under a huge tent. Heifers were judged in three separate age groups and in two separate categories: confirmation and grooming and handling. The judge had the contestants parade their heifer in a circle around him. In a series of halt and go commands, the judge made polite calls with the point of his finger.

"Thank you, you may be excused," he would say, pointing to those who are to be eliminated until he narrowed the field to three. Then came the good part. A yellow for third, a red for second and a blue ribbon for first place.

The judging started with the second oldest age group, which Pat and Gerald were in, and then they moved to the youngest age group, which my heifer was in. The full-grown cows were in the final group. In the confirmation judging, Pat and Gerald were both eliminated at the same time, just before the final three. When all the contestants returned for the grooming and handling competition, Pat was eliminated on the first call and Gerald won the yellow ribbon for third. He strutted a little, walking back to the tent and I could tell he was pretty proud.

I was feeling a little bit confident when my turn came. That's because throughout the day and the evening before, it seemed to me that all the adults walking through the barn seemed to stop and spend more time looking at my heifer than any of the others. I had to admit, she did look special. I sure hoped she was, because I wanted one of those ribbons like nothing I'd ever wanted before.

The judge eyed my heifer very carefully as I brought her into the circle and walked her around. Within a moment though he stopped looking at me and concentrated on my competition. We all stopped circling and stood at attention, under his calculating gaze. I took deep breaths each time the judge stopped to make a call. It seemed to take forever, but finally there were only three pairs left—and one of them was me and Little Bessie. Then there were two and I was still standing.

"Judging these animals is difficult, but my final call is an easy one," the judge announced to the crowd. "I could see it right off when these young heifers were brought out here. This young Holstein here," he said, pointing to Little Bessie, "is something special." I let out my breath and grinned. I'd done it! I'd won with a scrawny little gal who had been given to me as last choice.

The judge went on to explain in technical terms why my heifer was the blue ribbon winner. A huge smile on my face, tears creeping down my cheeks, I looked out to see my Ma, Dad, Gerald, and Pat all leading the applause. In the next session, for the judging of grooming and handling, the results were the same. I now had two blue ribbons! Better than I could have hoped for, especially when I first saw Little Bessie being led off my dad's trailer.

And, it wasn't even over yet. The three class winners were then brought out to decide the Grand Champion. One purple ribbon for confirmation and one purple ribbon for grooming and handling. In Ravenna, a purple ribbon trumped even a blue one, and I hadn't even dreamed of winning one of these.

The first round was for confirmation and one of the older heifers won that. But then came grooming and handling. Before I knew it, I had a purple ribbon in my hand to go with the two blue ones. I felt like a King when I led my Little Bessie in the parade through the midway in downtown Ravenna.

Boxing Brothers, Boxing Cousins

To us, our farm was home, and a whole lot of work; to our city relatives, it was more of a summer retreat. Well, for their kids it was, anyway. Our cousins from Muskegon came to stay with us every summer for a week or so at a time. One of my aunts or one of my uncles would talk to my dad about it late in the spring, saying how good the fresh country air was for youngsters and promising that niece or this nephew would help with chores. Sometimes it was David and Leo, sometimes other cousins.

Dad always said yes, and acted like the trade-off was a fair one, no matter how many times it didn't quite work out that way. Guaranteed, an hour or two of work on their first day with us was about all my Dad would get from them.

One time my mother's brother, Uncle Albert, sent his son, Al Jr., to our farm. On the day he arrived, the strawberries were ripe and he was hardly out of my uncle's car before he was assigned a row of strawberries to pick. We were all lined up out there in the strawberry patch, Ma, Lavern, Gerald, Junior and me, each with our heads down and fingers moving, advancing through our rows at different speeds. When we all ended up at the end of our rows, each of us had a full bucket of berries that Ma would make into jam and pies. Maybe even strawberry shortcake. All of us that is except Junior.

Junior had done as he was instructed and picked the vines clean, but only had a few berries rolling around in the bottom of his bucket. Maybe half a quart. What he did have was a mouth full of red stained teeth and a very full stomach. Another guest that summer, my cousin Roma, who was Ma's sister Evelyn's daughter, was even less help than Junior. Roma was my Mother's favorite, and a whiz of a student. She even won a prize at the Ravenna Fair's talent contest for reciting poetry. Something my brothers and I wouldn't have been caught dead doing for all the strawberries on Squires Road, but it sure impressed Ma. Roma wasn't much help around the farm, though. She didn't like the smell of cow manure.

Our most frequent visiting cousins were David and Leo, and I have to say that the four of us got along pretty well together, especially when we had some adventure or project on our minds. Still, there were disagreements. These were settled in what seemed to us to be a logical manner.

Whenever Gerald and Leo had an argument, they would put the Lobdell boxing gloves on and swing away at each other. My Dad bought the red gloves for just that purpose, and by the glee on his face anytime they were slid on, laced up, and put to use, there's no doubt he knew he was getting his money's worth out of them, many times over. My dad knew value when he saw it.

If Dad was busy working when the altercation occurred, Lavern would step in and referee in his place. He'd take up the job of announcer, promoter and corner man, too. Sometimes when Lavern was bored, I think he instigated arguments between cousins just because he felt like watching a boxing match. Though these matches were almost always between Gerald and Leo, who were evenly matched in size, there was one time that my cousin David and I put on those gloves. I don't even remember what our argument was about, but I do remember the sound of Lavern's announcer voice.

"In this corner of the ring," Lavern pointed to David and barked out, "weighing in at 105 pounds, Dandeee Daaaaaa-vid Benton." The tiny crowd made up of Gerald and Leo applauded and cheered. "And in this corner," he continued, pointing at me, "weighing in at 110 pounds, Wicked Waaaaaaaayne Lobdell!" The crowd cheered for me then and I puffed out my chest as far as it would puff.

"Gong!" Lavern yelled, to start our match.

I threw the first and last punch. My fist hit the side of David's face with a roundhouse right. A satisfying smacking sound had the crowd on its feet but David turned his head and walked away.

"Ladies and gentleman, that was a first round T-K-O!" Lavern shouted. The crowd cheered, David stomped off and threw down his gloves, but Lavern jerked my right arm in the air and gave me a congratulatory slap between my bare shoulder blades.

"Impressive, Wicked Wayne," he said.

I'm not sure if my big brother really was impressed with my boxing skills or just didn't want his show to end so soon, but he immediately suggested that I box cousin Leo. Confident with my first round TKO, I nodded to him that I was ready for the challenge. Leo, two years my senior and twenty pounds heavier, couldn't strap the gloves on fast enough. Lavern situated us each on either side of him, hollered "Gong!" and got out of the way.

Leo smacked me about three times before I knew what happened, his third punch landing square on my nose. It was my turn to throw off the gloves and walk away, but I had blood all over my nose and tears squirting out of my eyes. I was embarrassed, and wished no one had just seen my undoing. Man, I hated losing, and I was even more irked when I noticed that the audience witnessing my humiliation had just increased by one.

As I was exiting Lavern's make believe boxing arena, my cousin Rolland came riding up on his horse. Rolland was Dad's sister Mary's son, and while I didn't appreciate having anyone else see me get whupped, I suddenly had an idea to get back at Lavern for pumping me up to think that I could face Leo, and take the attention off my loss, in one fell swoop.

"Hey, how about if Lavern boxed Rolland?" I said to the group.

How could Lavern say no? I knew my brother and I knew he'd never walk away from a challenge. Rolland and Lavern were the same age, but they had never been friends. And, I knew that Rolland was a boxing fan himself, because he had bragged that he had been taking a few pointers from his dad. My plan worked.

Silently, they both entered the ring. Rolland, six feet tall and built like a basketball forward with wavy brown hair, was the quiet farm boy type. Lavern, at 5' 7" and built more like a running back, was the rambunctious wild one. One look at these two, and nobody was thinking about my loss to Leo anymore. For his part, Rolland looked especially pleased with my suggestion, relishing this chance to demonstrate all the moves his dad had taught him.

Leo elected himself the ring announcer, introducing both fighters. He didn't have the flair that Lavern did, but he got the job done.

Inside the ring, Rolland was grinning from ear to ear. Lavern was surprisingly quiet for a change. As soon as Leo yelled, "Gong," Rolland danced around the floor, mimicking the Friday night boxing style we had all seen on TV. He flicked out left jabs at Lavern and bobbed and weaved like Sugar Ray Robinson. Gerald, Leo, David, and I were all visibly impressed with Rolland's slick moves. We all gave him a ten out of ten for style.

Even though I still resented Lavern for instigating the fight I'd just lost, and even though I liked my cousin Rolland, deep down I still didn't want to see my older brother beaten. Lavern was my definition of tough, and I couldn't bear to have that idea shaken. Now though, it pained me to admit that he looked kind of pathetic next to the taller and longer-reaching Rolland.

Rolland danced around, but Lavern just stood there flat-footed, gloves up, and no expression at all on his face. I didn't know what to think – Lavern used to be my hero and it looked like he had no idea what to do. The only good thing that I could see was that with all his dancing around and flicking his hands back and forth, at least he wasn't getting close enough to Lavern to hit him.

"Are we gonna box or are you just gonna stand there?" Rolland taunted Lavern.

"Oh, are you ready for me to start?" asked Lavern.

"Show me your moves," commanded Rolland.

"Moves? Moves? I got a move for you." Lavern growled.

With that, Lavern bull-charged, his gloved hands swinging like a windmill in a hurricane. Before Rolland had a chance to show off the stylish moves he was so proud of, Lavern was all over him. Confused for the first time since walking into the ring, Rolland covered his face with his gloves and stumbled backwards across the barn floor. Lavern pawed at him in pursuit and Rolland ended up at the opposite end of the barn on his backside. He wasn't really hurt, just stunned.

"That's not boxing! We're supposed to move around and spar," Rolland protested.

"Yeah well, that's boxing to me. If you wanna dance, find yourself a girl. If you wanna duke it out, come get me," retorted Lavern.

Rolland stayed where he was. The boxing show was over.

Besides a flashy boxing style, Rolland also had a frisky riding horse that he called Big Red. With a shiny cinnamon-colored coat, Big Red looked just like a racehorse. Gerald and I had a horse too, Jenny. She was dark brown and overweight, closer to a plow horse than a racehorse. Jenny had a sweet personality and made a great pet, but if truth be told, she wasn't very exciting to ride. Still, Gerald and I did have one trick we liked to try with Jenny; we rode her under a low-hanging tree branch, reached up and swung up into the tree. Jenny was supposed to gallop away into the sunset while her rider disappeared high up on the tree's branches, just like Tonto did on TV. Jenny didn't get the trick though, and just stopped under the tree when her rider exited her back.

Today when I go horseback riding, I wouldn't dream of mounting up without a saddle; as a twelve year old though, I would gallop down the road, riding Jenny bare back, just like Tonto.

One day Rolland came over with Big Red to challenge Gerald to a race a half-mile down Squires Road to the next corner. I gave the "ready, set, go," sign and watched as Gerald and Jenny took up the challenge. Rolland and Big Red were at the finish line before Gerald and Jenny even got started. Gerald didn't have the heart to blame his loss on sweet Jenny, and instead claimed that Rolland jumped the start.

Where's the Calf?

When you hear someone say the words "swimming hole" they probably conjure up an image of a cool oasis, a secret spot with a grassy bank, clear water and a rope swing hanging from a thick tree branch, almost touching the surface. Somewhere, there probably are kids who had a swimming hole like that, but I wasn't one of them. On hot summer days, Gerald and I would ride our bikes to our swimming hole, but it wasn't anything like the one of country fantasy; it was just a hole in the ground filled with dirty water. A wide spot in a creek that my brother and I shared with ducks, turtles, water snakes, and bloodsuckers.

Three miles down the road and on private property, "our" swimming hole was cordoned off by an electric fence that ran right next to a sign that read "Private Property." The electric fence sounds scarier than it really was and we lost no time in scrambling under it. There was plenty of space between the ground and the first wire for a couple boys, anxious for a dip, to fit underneath. The electrified fence wasn't about to be a barrier to our fun as far as we were concerned; it was only a problem if you touched it, and neither one of us planned on ever doing that.

Until one day that is, when Gerald slipped. It was extra hot that day, and humid. Gerald and I were sweaty from doing our chores, and the farm dust stuck to our skin, gritty and itchy. As soon as we were finished with our work we didn't need to say a word to each other. We just jumped on our bikes and headed straight for the swimming hole.

The whole way there I was anticipating how good that murky water was going to feel. When we got to the spot, we leapt off our bikes, slid under the fence and jumped into the water. We splashed around for a while, churning up the silt and squirting water at each other. It felt so good, that neither one of us wanted to leave, but we didn't want to get caught or miss lunch either, so after a while we decided to head back home. We were crawling up out of the water and onto the slippery bank when Gerald reached up to grab my hand, but took hold of the fence wire instead.

"Help! Help!" he yelled out. He was soaking wet, the fence was full of enough juice to keep a cow contained, and he couldn't let go. The electric fence had him and had him good. We were alone, way out in a farmer's field and his only means of rescue was me. I had to do something fast. If I grabbed onto him, I'd get shocked too, but I certainly couldn't just leave him there frying. I decided right then and there to rescue my brother by sheer force. All one hundred pounds of me.

I took a running start and threw my body straight into Gerald shoulder first, knocking him off the fence, a couple feet in the air and flat on his backside. I had done my duty and freed him from the hold of the electric fence, but he landed on a rock, bruising his head. And something much more vulnerable too; his pride.

A bump on his head and a cut on his hand from the fence, not to mention having to be rescued by his little brother, didn't sit too well with Gerald. Once off the fence, he showed me all the loyalty of a water snake.

I took one look at his face and knew it would be a waste of time to ask if he was ok. Instead, I got on my bike and high-tailed it away as fast as I could, with my brother in hot pursuit yelling, "I'm gonna to kill you!"

Gerald was stronger and bigger than me, but I could run faster. I could also bike faster and I headed for home, beating him there. So much for cooling off at the swimming hole. By the time we both got back to the farm, we were winded, irritated, and hotter than we were when we left.

Several weeks passed before I was brave enough to go back to that swimming hole with Gerald. He never touched that fence again and I never got credit from him for my rescue. Not that I really expected it, but it still would have been nice. Thinking back, seems I made a pretty smart move knocking him away from his predicament. In my book, a bump to your pride and a bruise to your head are a lot better than being electrocuted, any day.

As years passed and Gerald and I grew up, he became increasingly resentful that people labeled me "the smart one in the family." What, he must have wondered, did that make him? I was faster and more coordinated too, and that day at the swimming hole was probably the first time I realized how hard that was to take for Gerald.

Gerald had me beat in another area though, just because he was older than me, and this irritated me just like my speed and smarts irritated him. Because I was younger, I was usually left out when our older cousins came to visit. Gerald, with two years on me, wasn't.

Sometimes, it worked out ok. Noticing that I was alone, Dad would ask me to be his helper, and not on scutt jobs either but on some fun projects. That's how I learned how to drive a tractor and I eventually became quite proficient at it. I learned how to back equipment into the tool shed—at the expense of smashing a hole in the side of the shed when I lost control one day. Despite my being shaken, Dad set aside his concern for the damage and insisted that I try again. Dad watched my successful second try. I think he was almost as proud of my maneuver as I was.

Cautious and thorough though he was, Dad occasionally made a mistake. These mistakes, whether big or small, were so rare during my boyhood that I can remember every one of them. Just like Big Buster with that poor heifer, this one involved a male cow, too. But this time it was just a young calf, not a full grown bull. Dad and I were hauling him to the Ravenna cattle auction to sell. Bull calves aren't very useful on a dairy farm.

Ravenna held a cattle auction every Saturday during the spring and summer. It was called a cattle auction but people brought other animals, too. Goats, sheep, chickens, ponies, mules, and anything else with four legs or two, that they didn't need and that some other farmer might.

People from miles away brought their livestock to sell, and the idea of going along with Dad to the auction sounded like a much better way to spend my day than being pushed around and taunted as the little outcast among the older boys. So when Dad suggested I go along, I didn't even hesitate.

Since they were butchered for veal, the bull calves were not actually auctioned off in the traditional sense, but rather sold in lots to the best daily bid. To get our bull calf from the field to the auction, Dad built a wood framed box stall that he could slide into the back of his pickup truck. His truck was old and rusty, with bad shocks and an ear-splitting muffler, but it got the job done. I would help him push the stall up a wooden ramp and into the back of the truck then help him lead the calf into the box stall. The calf would ride in there for the short trip to the auction.

This usually worked out just fine, and it would have this Saturday, too, if not for the airplane. Just after Dad and I finished first loading the stall into the pickup, and then loading the calf into the stall, we were distracted by a small airplane flying low over our farm.

Squires Road was an out of the way place and Ravenna was an out-of-the-way town, not on any major thoroughfare to anywhere. Planes not only never flew over our farm, they never flew anywhere near it. Dad pointed up and we watched for a few minutes as the airplane disappeared into the distance.

Dad and I thought little more about it and we hopped into the pickup and proceeded the few miles on to the auction. Pulling in, we stopped at the drive-up booth to check in our bull calf with the attendant.

"What ya need?" The man in the booth asked Dad impatiently.

"What does it look like?" Dad fired back. Given that my Dad had been to this same spot for this same purpose and talked to this same guy many times, "What ya need?" didn't seem like a logical, or polite, question to him.

"Don't look like much to me," came back the response.

"Not your job to judge what I brought," my dad countered. " Just give me my receipt." I had heard that tone in his voice before, and it was usually when one of my brothers or I had been bold enough to backtalk him.

"Don't get smart with me. Now, move your dam truck."

Red faced, Dad jumped out of his truck looking like he was ready to go after the attendant right in his booth.

"What to hell? Jesus Christ, my calf is gone!" yelled Dad.

I looked back and saw he was right. The bed of the pickup was empty. It took us both a minute to realize that after loading the stall and calf back home we were so distracted by the low flying airplane that neither one of us had closed the tailgate. Dad's custom box stall had worked its way off the back of the truck, calf and all. Its noisy muffler was loud enough to cover up the sound of a hardwood stall and a calf crashing onto the pavement.

For me, this was exciting but Dad was frantic – heaven only knew where we dropped that calf and where he was now. Losing the calf meant losing some income that we were counting on. Plus, Dad hated to think of any animal suffering needlessly. He apologized to the attendant, and jumped back into the truck.

With one of us focused and worried and one of us focused and excited, Dad and I were off on an adventure to find a calf on the loose. We backtracked through town. I looked to the right and Dad looked to the left. For the first time since I can remember, Dad didn't take the time to remind me we were passing over "Grandpa Lobdell's bridge." After the bridge, we turned left up the hill back toward our farm. The box stall was big and couldn't be far off the road, but we hadn't seen a single sign of it. The calf could be anywhere.

Finally, halfway home, just before a curve in the road, there was the box stall, sitting in the middle of the road. Much to our amazement, the calf was still in it. Neither of us could imagine how the box fell off and the calf stayed in, but there it was.

My Dad took about a half a second to relish his relief, and then we reloaded the stall and calf, made sure the tailgate was closed and returned to the auction. Dad apologized to the attendant again, picked up his receipt which he turned in for a check, then bought me a Fudgesicle at one of the snack stands before we headed for home. Our work for the day might have been done, but we had a story we could tell a hundred times.

Rocky

My dad worked so much and so hard that he had very little free time to spend with Gerald and me. The one consistent exception to this was Friday Night Fights on TV. We'd all gather around our little black and white television set, move the antenna around this way and that until the picture was as clear as we could make it, and sit back and watch the fights together.

We had our favorite fighters; Rocky Graziano, Gene Fullmer, and our number one all-time favorite, Rocky Marciano. We were always disappointed that the championship fights were not televised. Radio broadcast had to do. The night Rocky Marciano fought Jersey Joe Wolcott in September of 1952, we were sure Rocky was going to lay Jersey Joe out.

As the bell rang for round one, Dad leaned foreword in his chair, holding up his right hand to show us he had his fingers crossed.

Rocky was undefeated; forty-three wins, thirty-seven by knockout. Wolcott was a great champion and a great boxer, but nearing the end of his career. We sat down to listen to the fight, ready to hear Rocky knock him out in short order.

"Oh no! Get up, Rocky. Get up!" we cried to each other, when Rocky hit the canvas in the first round. He had never been down before. How could this happen?

Rocky rose to his feet quickly like the scrapper he was. We sat silent in our chairs for the rest of the fight, listening as Wolcott gave Rocky Marciano a boxing lesson, round after round.

Rocky was bleeding around the eyes and staggered several times. Dad sat on the edge of his chair, leaning foreword, jerking his arms around as if trying to help Rocky.

"Looks like Marciano is finished," said the announcer. "He has blood over his eyes, but he just won't go down. They'll have to stop this fight."

The boxers went to their respective corners after round twelve. "Rocky's manager, Al Weil, has just told Marciano that he may have to throw in the towel," said the announcer.

The Wolcott boxing lesson continued at the beginning of round thirteen. Then, suddenly, the announcer let out with a yell.

"Wolcott is down! Wolcott is down! Jersey Joe Wolcott is on his back! Rocky landed a vicious right on the jaw of Jersey Joe. Seven, eight. He is not getting up. Ten. The fight is over! Rocky Marciano is the new world's heavyweight champion!"

We three Lobdell men were all on our feet, jumping up and down, hugging each other, Dad holding up his right hand. "Crossing my fingers, that's what did it," he boasted with a broad grin.

We listened to the post fight interviews of Rocky and Wolcott, and the sports announcers' commentary for a while, and then went to bed. I don't know about my dad, but Gerald and I couldn't get to sleep for hours.

Throughout that winter, while watching the Friday night fights, we talked about the grudge match planned between Marciano and Wolcott. The date was set in April of 1953. We looked forward to that for months, shadow boxing on our way to school and pretending to be Rocky and Jersey Joe in the back yard at home. Then one day in early April we were given the thrill of our lives.

"How would you boys like to meet Rocky Marciano tomorrow?" My dad said to Gerald and me.

The idea of actually getting to meet our hero was unfathomable, and we were sure Dad was just pulling our leg. As it turned out, he was not. Rocky Marciano was in training fifteen miles away at a training facility set up at the Holland Furnace Company in Holland, Michigan. Our dad was taking an afternoon off to take us to see Rocky. He would pick us up at Hoogstraat at noon the very next day. Our teacher, Mrs. Lindgren, was all too happy to excuse us for the afternoon.

All morning, Gerald and I watched the clock on the schoolhouse wall. Just as planned, at exactly noon Dad pulled up in front of the school in his pickup truck. We closed our books and dashed for the door, but when we saw him waiting for us, our hearts dropped.

Our foster sister, Pat, and one of her high school girlfriends were in the front cab with my Dad. Sitting primly in spots that rightly should have been ours. Our excitement melted like an ice cube in the sun. Two giggling girls who hardly knew who Rocky Marciano was, cared nothing about boxing, and just wanted an afternoon off from school, had the best seats in the house. At least for now. Gerald and I, as big as boxing fans as ever there was, would have to ride in the back. Usually, that wouldn't have been a big deal. We'd both ridden in the back lots of times. The big deal was not having this special day with our Dad all to ourselves.

Every drop of disappointment drained away from Gerald and me when we stepped inside that training center. Despite the Pat invasion, the day was a thrill. We watched Rocky pound the punching bag with awesome power and batter sparing partners around the ring. We even got his autograph. Patricia and her friend spent most of their time standing around, giggling and covering their mouths with their hands, but we hardly noticed.

The Marciano-Wolcott return match, scheduled for April 10, 1953 was postponed until May 15, after Marciano had a training injury. For true boxing fans like the Lobdell men, the wait was worth it. Rocky Marciano knocked Wolcott out in the first round. During the broadcast, Pat was off in her bedroom, listening to music with her friend. Dad, Gerald and I nervously hovered over the radio, jumping for joy at the sudden ending. Rocky was King.

"It was an Accident!"

The age fourteen is often the age of muscle maturity. It certainly was for my brother Gerald and as he began to feel those developing muscles I became the target. I can understand why. I seemed to be everybody's favorite. Adults made comments that I was the smart one in the family. A few of my Dad's friends came to our farm to go pheasant hunting and, much to the chagrin of Gerald; they picked me to go with them. One of our neighbors needed somebody to help with his chores, for pay. He picked me. I seemed to be first to get everything. Of course it was unfair, but what would any twelve year old do?

Although I was faster, Gerald had one big advantage. Two years more mature, he was stronger and, believe me, he let me know it. Much of my time was spent with him alone, just Gerald and me. Gerald seemed to be able to make himself feel better by shoving me, punching me, or just ordering me around. Occasionally, I would fight back, but he was too much bigger and stronger. My best chance was to pretend I was Sugar Ray Robinson and dance around him, occasionally landing a jab. If my Dad saw us fighting, he would just watch. My mother, on the other hand, would usually scream out orders to my dad.

"Howard, stop em! Stop em right now. They shouldn't fight." My dad would watch for a few minutes and then stop us. He always thought "a little scrap" between boys, and especially between brothers, was just part of growing up.

Although my mother complained often, my dad and she rarely engaged in a serious argument. The routine was for my mother to complain enough for my dad to either give in, or become perturbed and just say, "I don't want to hear about it anymore." And, that would end the discussion.

An exception to that routine came when my Dad brought home two .22 caliber pump guns. They were used guns that he bought, where else, but at an auction. The purpose of the guns was to shoot squirrels and birds. The gun operated off of air pressure, the power level was determined by how much air was pumped in before pulling the trigger. We were warned to not pump more than three times, which provided adequate power to kill a bird, chipmunk, or squirrel. My mother was afraid of the guns and verbally battled my dad for days over them, disregarding his command to, "stop bitching about those harmless little guns." Gerald and I were thrilled with the guns and promised Ma that we would be careful.

A few days after Dad brought them home, it must have been around 8:00 or 9:00 in the evening, just before dark. I remember the sun dropping down beyond the treetops and Gerald and I were in the back woods of our eighty-acre farm. I had scored my first squirrel kill. We had both taken out some birds, but that was the first squirrel for either of us. I was first again.

While leaning quietly against a tree, looking for another shot, I felt a jolting sting in the side of my head. I saw stars and planets, and not because I was looking up at the sky. Surprisingly, I didn't feel much pain. I reached my hand up to feel the spot just above my ear where I'd felt the sting. There was blood there and then I felt a pellet that had lodged into the side of my head.

"It was an accident, an accident." Gerald came rushing to me. "My gun went off by accident."

Gerald reached his own hand up to the area above my ear and pulled the pellet from the side of my head. Amazingly, the pellet had struck me just above the ear between two bones, only penetrating about a half inch into my flesh. The bleeding was minimal. Gerald was more frightened I think than I was.

"Now listen, if Ma and Dad find out, they will take our rifles away," Gerald warned me, in his commanding manner. I agreed. Not only did I not want to lose my rifle, I was intimidated with the possibility of Gerald's revenge if I dared tell.

At the time of the incident and forever after, I could not conceive in my mind how that accident happened. One good thing came out of it; Gerald was very good to me for quite some time after that. The small injury was not very visible and healed over with only a tiny scar. Ma and Dad were never told of the injury. In fact, this is the first time I ever revealed this story. I prefer to think of the good times Gerald and I had together; the many years of exploring the country side, snitching Wally Wagoner's apples and going to the Ravenna Fair.

Wayne at Hoogstraat in 1949, Jacqueline middle left, Gerald
second from top left, Wayne middle row second from right,
and teacher Garnet Lindgren.

Wayne on a tractor, age 12.

Wayne at Ravenna Fair with
champion heifer in 1952.

Dark Days

Not So Tough, Anymore

A red Cadillac convertible was pulling into our yard. Somebody must be lost. I had seen pictures of fancy convertibles like this one but never once did I imagine someone coming to see us in a car like that.

It was a warm afternoon in September, a few days after the Marciano-Wolcott fight. I was sitting on my bike in the front yard, about to head out to my friend Ronald's house, so it must have been a Saturday.

Two men were in the car. I saw the passenger first as the car slowly pulled into our driveway. He was wearing a clean white shirt, had dark curly hair, and I could just tell he was a city guy. Then the driver opened the door and bounced out. I was stunned; it was Lavern. A year and a half had gone by since I'd seen him, but my brother was alive. I lay down my bike and walked toward him.

"Hi, little brother. Boy, you're getting big," he barked out as he approached me. "You ready to take on your big brother?" He put up his dukes and shadow boxed around me.

I just smiled. I couldn't believe it, it was really him.

"Ma! Ma! It's Lavern!" I yelled toward the house.

My mother came out, stood on the porch, and froze. She put her hands to her face.

"Oh my God! Oh my God, my prayers have been answered!"

Ma walked down the steps crying. Lavern gave her a little hug and then stepped back "You don't need to cry," he said, looking away.

Just then, Dad and Gerald came walking up. Their mouths were hanging open. Gerald looked at Lavern and then at the Cadillac. Dad was quivering. Mr. "tough as nails" wasn't so tough anymore. I saw my dad just then as Lavern must have seen him. Skinny, tired-looking, and even weak.

In the past few weeks, Ma had been telling him that he should see a doctor. Dad had lost a lot of weight recently and sometimes when he thought no one was looking, he could be seen grimacing, as if fighting off some mysterious pain. He was just past forty, but he looked more like sixty. My dad broke down along with my mother. They both hugged Lavern and then hugged each other.

"What do you think of the new wheels I got here, Dad?" Lavern finally asked. Both he and his slick-looking passenger were uncomfortable, I could tell. Lavern kept looking down at the ground, up at the sky, across the street. Anywhere but into my parents' faces. Gerald and I were uncomfortable, too. Patricia was still living with us and she just stood in the background; she had heard of Lavern but never met him. He had disappeared before she came to the farm.

Dad didn't know what to say about the flashy car, and so Lavern introduced us all to the city man he had with him. His name was Mr. Jerry Gutnick and he was the sales director for the magazine company that Lavern worked for. That made him Lavern's boss and, Lavern admitted sheepishly, the owner of the big red car.

"Boys, why don't you take Mr. Gutnick here on a tour of the barn," Dad said to Gerald and me. "City guys love to see barns, don't they Mr. Gutnick?"

The three of us knew that sending us off was just a way for Ma and Dad to talk to Lavern all alone, but we played along. My parents were so shocked to see Lavern, it had taken a few minutes for their anger over his abrupt disappearance to surface, but now it was there. I can only imagine the lecture Lavern got from the two of them and what excuses he had stored up for not contacting them even once over the past year and a half.

My oldest brother had come home, but he stayed only one night. The whole family stayed up late listening to Lavern's traveling tales and we told him all about meeting Rocky Marciano. He left the next day, saying that he had to work over in Muskegon, but he promised to call in a few days. We didn't hear from him for a week or more. When he did call, he said he was in Detroit, had quit his job, and wanted to come home. He just needed money for a bus ticket. Of course my Dad sent him the money, but Lavern never showed up. He was gone again.

Looking back, it seems to me that my Dad's main activity was struggling, with a few happy times thrown in here and there. His labor in the foundry and on the farm was so long and so rough, and his progress so small and so hard won.

Like a Fallen Apple

Our farm had one ancient broken down apple tree in the front yard, and I think of it sometimes. It had grown there for decades, but had the worst luck with apples. In the spring, it was covered with blossoms, it grew apples that gradually ripened and came into full fruit, but then quickly shriveled up and fell to the ground inedible. Our life, and our Dad, were each falling apart after blossoming for a while, just like the fruit on that tree.

My Dad was getting sicker. He wasn't strong enough to keep up the farm the way he wanted to, and worrying about Lavern sapped what little strength he did have. A gray fog seemed to follow him everywhere. He eventually didn't even get out of bed. Back then they called it a nervous breakdown. Dad's mind was sad and broken, but his body had a breakdown, too. He was convinced that he was dying. He was hospitalized and his anguish was advanced enough that the doctors recommended electroshock treatments. They seemed to help, but there was more bad news. Dad had TB.

All those years breathing in soot at Lakey's Foundry had coated his lungs with black, smoky bacteria. Dad's body had been fighting the illness for years but no one realized it. Neighbors helped with the farm. Gerald and I did what we could, but we were just kids. Shep, our wonder dog, was hit by a car and killed. Uncle Alfred moved out and rented a house in Muskegon. Our foster sister Pat turned sixteen, found a boyfriend, and moved back in with her mother. We only ever saw her a couple times after that.

The end of the farm was coming; we knew it had arrived when Paul Morley came to inspect our property. The devil himself might as well have been poking around inside our barn and walking our fields.

Gerald turned sixteen, quit school in the middle of seventh grade, moved in with Uncle Alfred, and tried to find a job. He couldn't read, so he'd bring the applications to Uncle Alfred to fill out for him. Garnet Lindgren, our Hoogstraat teacher, had written Gerald off as a troublemaker long ago and never taught him to read. She just assumed he couldn't learn and moved him along from grade to grade.

When Gerald finally found a job as an usher in a downtown movie theater, the first person I told was Mrs. Lindgren. I was fourteen and in the seventh grade at Hoogstraat and she was still my teacher. She gave me a strange look and said, "You must mean he got a job as a janitor."

The farm was sold to Mr. Morley. All our animals, the tractor I'd learned to drive, and our other machinery was auctioned off. Dad was moved into a TB sanitarium. They said he would be there for two to three years. Mr. Morley cut our farm in half, and sold the pieces to two of our old neighbors, Mr. Link and Mr. May. My mother and I were all that was left. The sale included the provision that Ma and I could stay on the farm for a year, so at least we weren't homeless.

Without the animals or the crops, there wasn't much to do but go visit Dad. The TB hospital was twenty miles away though, and Ma couldn't drive, so I qualified for a special driving permit. Twice a week I drove Ma to visit Dad at the TB hospital. I was fourteen.

Visiting my Dad was harder work than anything I ever did on the farm. I wanted to see him, but not like he was; pale and weighing at most a hundred pounds. He was always sad. Once I told him something that seemed to invigorate him a little. Mr. May, our neighbor, had to travel south to Kentucky for a family matter and was paying me $20 to tend to his farm for the four days that he'd be gone. Dad acted pleased, even smiling a little.

"I want you to do all the things Mr. May asks you to do, and then I want you to look around for anything extra you can see to do to help him," he said.

"Sure Dad." I said, not really getting the picture. But before my Ma and I left, Dad repeated his instructions to me. Even broken down, sick, lungs black, and heart defeated, Howard Lobdell was still hard at work. It might have been through me from his hospital bed, but my dad was still working.

Two days later, I commenced what was to be my first management job; taking care of Mr. May's farm. There wasn't a lot to manage. He only had four cows, a young heifer, three pigs, and some chickens. Milking the cows, feeding the animals, and gathering the eggs only took two to three hours each day. Remembering what my father advised, however, I looked around for an extra project. My eyes landed on the heifer.

She was housed in a box stall that needed some serious work. Cows or heifers are placed in stalls with straw on the floor. Every day a little fresh straw is added to the stall for bedding. The accumulation of urine and manure and straw, when aged in the field, makes good fertilizer. Placing fresh straw in the stall also keeps the animal from walking and lying in a dirty pen.

A farmer's most dreaded and dirty chore is to clean out the box stall. It's not a hard job, but it is a dirty one. You put on a pair of boots, used a pitchfork to pitch the matted piles of straw into a wheelbarrow, rolled the full wheelbarrow out into a manure pile somewhere in the barnyard. There, the manure accumulates and ages until its ready to be moved to the fields.

Efficient farmers clean out their box stalls after the bedding is about two to three feet high. My Dad would never allow one to build up beyond even two feet. Mr. May's box stall had accumulated about six feet of manure. Another week or so and that poor heifer would be bumping her head on the ceiling. I would guess I worked about four hours one day and four the next to clean out that stall. When Mr. May came home, he was flabbergasted.

"Wayne, I spent the whole trip home dreading that job," he said. Even better, he gave $5 extra and complemented me on my work ethic every time he saw me for the next twenty years. I didn't think to tell him that it came by way of my Dad.

Mr. May told other farmers about me and they offered me jobs, too. On my next visit to the hospital, I made my Dad's day when I told him about cleaning that dirty box stall. He said that he wished he didn't have to sell the farm, so that I could take it over someday.

The final few months of seventh grade was a sad time for me. Besides my lonely Ma, my sick Dad, our ruined farm, and being separated from my brothers, I was still a teenager and wanted to have friends and have fun, just like the other kids I knew.

Ronald and Jacqueline Jablonski would be finishing eighth grade and moving on to Ravenna high school. I'd be stuck at Hoogstraat with nobody but the one other eighth grader, Janet Shook, for company. And she was the teacher's pet. No more Ronald to smoke Chesterfield cigarettes with. No more Jacqueline to look at. A whole year with just prissy old Mrs. Lindgren and Janet Shook with her mouth full of braces, and me.

After school, it wasn't any better. Home alone with my mother and nothing to do. No Shep, no Gerald, no swimming hole, no Jenny the plow horse. No nothing.

And that's how it was, too, for the next couple months. With nothing better in the offing, I decided, for the first time ever, to do my homework. By that time in my educational career, I had been in school for nine years. With a little extra effort, I was able to surprise Mrs. Lindgren with my test scores and I finished seventh grade in a flurry of A's.

I decided that getting all A's was kinda fun. Ma and Dad boasted to their friends that I would become a high school graduate someday. Maybe I would even go to college and become a teacher, they said. I was not interested in that. The only teachers I knew were Mrs. Lindgren and her one year replacement, Mrs. Bennett – not exactly role models.

My First Move

The most exciting day of that year came when Mrs. Lindgren decided to take Janet Shook and me, as seventh graders, with the graduating eighth grade class for their special field trip to Muskegon. We visited the dairy that Mrs. Lindgren's husband was a partner in, took a tour of the beach, then returned home in the evening. The exciting part was all eight students riding in the back of Mr. Lindgren's van.

We were in tight quarters. On the trip to Muskegon, I sat next to my friend Ronald. With some careful timing on my part, on the return trip home, I managed to be seated next to Jacqueline Jablonski. There I was, shoulder to shoulder with Jacqueline and it was getting dark. After all those years of admiring her, I was finally having an actual conversation with her—and, I felt, doing quite well with it.

About half way home, I got brave. I knew it was a risky move, but this was my chance of a lifetime. I very carefully and slowly moved my right arm around Jacqueline's shoulder. I held my breath, anticipating rejection. After all, many others, including my friend Ronald, were seated in full view of my bold risk. I glanced at her out of the corner of my eye. She smiled.

My arm remained comfortably on Jacqueline's shoulder for the remainder of the trip. Nothing was said about it. We all just chatted as if nothing was going on. And of course, nothing of significance was going on, at least to anyone but Jacqueline and me. I suspect that was the first time a boy placed his arm on her shoulder. It certainly was my first advance toward a girl.

I lay awake that night, excited but sad. Jacqueline had allowed me to put my arm around her, yet she was off to high school and I would still be at Hoogstraat. I kicked myself for misbehaving in fifth grade.

A Family No More

Our financial status was deteriorating, Ma's and mine. My mother decided that she would stay with me on the farm for the summer, making money picking fruit, and then she'd move to Muskegon to find a full time job. I would move in with my dad's sister and her husband, Aunt Mary and Uncle Ken. Their son Rolland had left home to join the Army.

If we were poor, they were poorer, but Aunt Mary wanted to help and wanted the company. Plus, they lived in Ravenna and I didn't want to leave, so the plan was for me to live with them and finish Hoogstraat and then go on to Ravenna High School. My mother moved to Muskegon to live at my Uncle Alfred's apartment while she trained to become a nurse's aide. Aunt Mary and Uncle Ken were kind to me, but I sure got tired of bean soup and baked potatoes. Whenever Uncle Ken brought home money, we had good food and Aunt Mary was an excellent cook, but when the money ran out, it was bean soup and potatoes.

Howard and Marion Lobdell's family was no longer a family. The only member old enough and healthy enough to be of any real help, Lavern, became a liability instead of an asset. My mother got a call from him that summer. He was in South Bend, Indiana, and in jail. In order to get out, he needed money to pay a fine for selling magazines without a permit.

My mother sent him the money without telling my father. In fact, she did tell him something but it was the opposite of the truth. She told my dad that she got a call from Lavern and that he was doing fine and would be coming home soon. Dad kept waiting and asking, but of course, Lavern never came.

In the summer of 1955 I was booked up daily with hourly farm jobs with our neighbor, Mr. May. He paid me 75 cents an hour, up from the 50 cents he had paid me the previous year. Mrs. May fixed my lunch and came to me several times a day saying, "time for a pop break." The first time I heard her call that out, I was excited, then mildly disappointed. Her "pop" was really just Kool Aid.

One day I got a call from a man who was the farm foreman for the area's largest dairy farmer, Mr. Donald Nutt. He had heard about my work and offered me $1 an hour to load hay on wagons. I was proud to tell my dad that I had a job working for Mr. Nutt. But my best job that summer was working for Mr. Shook, my classmate Janet's dad. Not only were Mr. and Mrs. Shook the nicest farmers I had ever worked for, they paid me $1.25 an hour and provided me with a feast at lunchtime.

A side benefit of the job was that Janet, braces now gone, was looking pretty good. She always gave me a friendly smile, but usually had little to say. While working, I would look up to see her riding around the farm on her horse. Janet, an only child, kept busy with horseback riding and ballet lessons. She was not expected to work.

The Raffle

After a summer of working and saving and helping Ma out with the household bills, I had enough money left over to buy myself a new three-speed bike. When school started, I rode that bike a mile and a half from Aunt Mary's to and from school, as well as home and back for lunch. It felt good to know that I paid for my transportation myself.

Throughout eighth grade, Janet was still my only classmate, and we competed for the honor of best class performance. I knew she was smart and favored by Mrs. Lindgren, but our assignments were not all that challenging, so keeping up with her was pretty easy.

A raffle ticket-selling contest in the fall of 1955 pitted Janet and me against each other. I don't even remember what the prize was, just the competition. Proceeds were to be used for new school supplies. A secret prize would be awarded to the student who sold the most tickets.

Janet had an advantage over me, she thought. She could ride her horse all around the countryside, selling tickets door to door, and was clearly the expected winner. Other students made little effort, knowing that competing with Janet would be futile. Janet sold her initial supply in one day. But so did I. She might have had a horse, but I had my new bike.

As each week went by, Mrs. Lindgren reported to the class that Janet and I were way out front. We sold many times more of those tickets than all the other students put together. As the numbers climbed, I became more and more determined to come out on top, riding my bike as far as ten miles away.

With a week to go, I was leading comfortably enough to develop a winning strategy. I held back some sold tickets on my report. I knew Janet would come with a final week rally and wanted to make sure I topped it. Not only that, I bought some tickets with my own money and convinced my mother to buy some too. I had a big number ready for my final report. After Janet turned in her final sales report, I knew

I had her beat by a wide margin and proudly turned mine in. I had beaten the teacher's pet.

"We have a tie," said Mrs. Lindgren, when she announced the final tally to the class. "Janet and Wayne have both worked so hard we are going to split the prize." The actual numbers of tickets we each sold were never announced.

I smiled and accepted the prize, though to this day I can't for the life of me remember what it was. Inside, I was furious. I was the winner and wasn't getting credit for it. The prize didn't even matter to me; only winning mattered and Mrs. Lindgren called it a tie. Of course, Mrs. Lindgren was probably right, and we both deserved to win. But, I sure didn't feel that way at the time.

Uncle Alf's

I walked slowly up the rickety unlit stairway in Uncle Alfred's little house. A light fixture hung from the pitched roof ceiling. One small window, next to the framed bed, gave me a view out at the boarded up house next door. The wood floor was full of squeaks; the ceiling only high enough for me to stand in the middle of the room. This was to be my room. The first floor included two bedrooms, a bathroom, and a kitchen that opened into a living room with a couch, two lounge chairs, and a TV in the corner.

The house, wood framed, had a drab look with its painted grey siding and charcoal roof tiles and a very old oak tree dominated the space in the middle of the small front yard, its branches hanging over the house. A dirt driveway led from the road past the house to a dilapidated shed in back.

This would be my home for the summer.

My Hoogstraat years were over. I planned to return to Aunt Mary and Uncle Ken's in the fall to attend Ravenna High School. First though, I was supposed to find work and experience the city.

My new surroundings felt strange and uncomfortable. Homes close together, needing paint, and old broken down cars sitting in yards. I wasn't concerned about the smell of city air; I only noticed that it was different.

Taking a closer look out my new bedroom window, I could see two little boys kicking a ball in the street. Suddenly, they picked up their ball and ran away as three teens dressed in Levis and T-shirts walked boldly down the street toward them, yelling something as they came closer. Strutting like the Gestapo, they were all smoking. Each of them had a pack of cigarettes rolled up in his T-shirt sleeve, bunched up at the shoulder. I had heard about city gangs and wondered if I had just seen my first gang members.

"What you looking at, punk?" were his first words. As a farm boy, I wasn't sure what a punk was, but assumed that it wasn't a compliment. It was about 9 the next morning and I was sitting on the porch steps, thinking about where to look for a job, when he walked by. This was one of the three that I had seen out my window the previous evening. Apprehensive and not sure how to react, I rose from my seat.

"Hi, I just moved here yesterday afternoon. I don't know anybody around here."

"Come here" Larry ordered. I obeyed. As I approached, he gave me a shove with his right hand against my chest. I backpedaled only about a half step, not losing my balance. I was fully-grown at 15, 5' 7" and 155 lbs. Farm labor combined with the genes of stocky Lobdells had made me into an exceptionally strong teenager.

Larry was an inch taller and a lot heavier than me. He had long wavy hair which made him look older than me, even though I found out later we were the same age. I don't remember feeling fear of him at that moment. I did feel disappointment. I needed a friend. I also noticed that he seemed to be a bit surprised at what little impact his shove had on me.

"You need to know boy, that me and my friends run this neighborhood. Nobody messes with us around here and when school starts, nobody messes with us there either. Not the spics, not the niggers, not the jocks. You got that?"

"Sure, good to meet you." I hoped I said the right thing.

"You look like a pretty husky guy. We might let you join us if you do what we say."

This was my lucky day—I thought. I had been worried about the neighborhood. If I could make friends with Larry, I could be safe and have someone to tell me what to do in this unfamiliar territory.

"Have a smoke. Name's Larry. Yours?"

"Wayne," I responded as Larry lit the cigarette he handed to me.

"Be cool. Gotta meet the boys now. I'll be back to see ya." Larry walked away.

A Job in the City

The fruit market, called simply M46 Market, provided a breath of air. Mr. Patterson, the market owner, reminded me of Mr. May, our neighbor on the farm and my previous boss. Mr. Patterson was about 5' 9", slightly plump, had a friendly smile and a receding hairline.

"You're hired," he proclaimed, after I helped him unload a potato delivery. On the same morning after meeting Larry, I had stopped in at the market to ask if they had a job opening. Mr. Patterson was working up a sweat, personally unloading the delivery because his helper didn't show up for work that morning. Lucky me, I just offered to help and ended up with the job. He was impressed when I told him about my work experience on the farm.

"Farm boy, just what I need," he said. These city kids around here don't know what work is all about."

He was right. The other two teenagers that he had working for him were always last minute arriving to work and out of there one minute after the scheduled quitting time. Their work attitude didn't make sense. I couldn't understand why someone would be late for work, let alone just not show up. And, when they were on the job, why would they do the least amount of work they could get away with? The only day those two guys seemed happy was payday. They yakked all day about how they were going to spend their paycheck.

My new job was only part time, from 7 a.m. to 11 a.m., six days a week. Consequently, while looking and waiting to find a second job, I had lots of time to get to know my new friend. Larry came to my house two days later. He was impressed that I had been hired at the M46 Market and would have money to spend.

The more I came to know Larry, the more I began to realize that he and his friends, Johnny and Donnie, were strange. Getting together with Larry was always an adventure. I felt myself being pulled into a new world.

Trouble with Larry

Larry Chevrino looked out his bedroom window to see a Muskegon Police car pull into his driveway. One hour earlier we had each grabbed three bottles of Coke off a truck that was making a delivery to a local grocery store. We each drank one, gave one to Larry's Mom, and put the others in the refrigerator.

I was surprised when Larry's Mom didn't ask where the Coke came from. Actually, I didn't like Larry's idea all that much, but, "come on don't be a chicken," was all it took to get me to participate.

Larry was my only friend in the neighborhood. Ma was now working as a nurse's aide. Brother Gerald spent his time on whatever odd job he could find, and hanging out with Cousin Leo. Uncle Alfred was still complaining of pain and unable to work. I am not sure where he got money to pay his rent and buy food, probably some type of government assistance. From what I recall from his days on the farm, he had always been sickly and his only job had been two years on the WPA, a Franklin Roosevelt program to help the poor.

Larry lived alone with his mom in a four-plex apartment, just six blocks away from me. The two bedroom apartments all looked alike, painted beige with a concrete porch and steps in front where a narrow strip of burned out grass separated the apartment from the sidewalk and the street.

"Jimmy Green, that God damn Jimmy Green, he saw us and ratted," Larry yelled. "We're gonna get that little shit and kick his ass." Larry was mumbling insults as he climbed back to the top of his bunk bed. I was occupying the lower bunk.

I was frightened, heart pounding, thoughts of having to go to jail, wondering what my dad would say. Dad, now nearing the end of his stay in the TB Sanitarium, was gaining weight and gaining confidence. As I lay in Larry's bunk bed, Dad's warning words from two years ago came back to me.

"I'm going to be in this hospital a long time; not sure if I will make it. Your Uncle Alfred's neighborhood isn't so good. There are bad kids around there. Be careful when you go there; don't get in any trouble with those kids."

From the temporary comfort and safety of Larry's room I could hear his mom answer the door for the policemen. I walked around in a circle, looking up at Larry, who was just lying on his upper bunk with a grin on his face. Why wasn't he worried like me? We were in serious trouble, I was sure of it.

I could hardly hear what the police were saying, but I could sure hear Mrs. Chevrino's loud voice. "Larry and his friend been here all afternoon. They don't got any pop. Why you cops always picking on Larry. He don't steal. No, you can't talk to him. Get a warrant if you think you got proof to arrest him."

Larry was up on his bunk smiling, I could feel it. I was rooting for Mrs. Chevrino, but not expecting her to prevail over the police. They did go away that day but I was scared for a week, just waiting for them to come to my door. They never did. Apparently they either didn't have the proof or had more important things to do. I was amazed that afternoon that Larry's Mom never had a thing to say to him about it.

The week of my first ever theft was made worse when Larry decided I should be assigned to punch out Jimmy Green, the so called "rat."

One look at skinny little Jimmy and I protested to Larry, "I can't punch that little guy, it wouldn't be fair."

I don't think Larry understood the meaning of fair. He definitely didn't like my rejecting his order.

"Ok, here's the deal farm boy," Larry blurted, "come with me. We're gonna wrestle. Deal is I take you down in two minutes or less; you have to punch Jimmy Green out. Deal?"

"Deal," I answered, thinking this was my out of an assignment I didn't want. About ten seconds later I had Larry Chevrino on the ground, sitting on top of him. I now had earned some respect from Larry and his two buddies, Johnny and Ron, but my comfort with our activities was not improving. My first real Jackson Hill neighborhood fist fight leaves me with a memory that I still wish I could erase.

My baseball bat was stolen from where I had left it lying on the front porch of Uncle Alfred's house. Larry and Johnny informed me that my bat was stolen by a boy named Arthur Rice. My brother

Gerald confirmed that he too had heard that Arthur had taken my bat. I now had a commitment to revenge, to defend my honor.

On a Sunday afternoon, while searching the help wanted section of the Muskegon Chronicle, I was interrupted by Larry, Johnny and Gerald.

"He's at the basketball court. Arthur is, the kid who stole your bat."

One single thought entered my mind, I had to fight this guy, whoever he was.

The basketball court was about six blocks away. Arthur was in a three on three pick up basketball game. My heart pounding, I walked onto the basketball court and confronted Arthur. The game stopped. They all saw trouble.

"You stole my bat." I looked up at Arthur, a tall and slim kid with hair hanging in his long boney face. Sweat running down his face, Arthur stood up to me boldly. I am sure he was frightened, but too proud to walk away with his friends watching.

"I don't know anything about your bat," he growled loudly and edged closer to me. As if to intimidate me with his height.

He came too close. Without hesitation and out of a feeling of obligation, I unleashed a right hand punch. I was aiming at his jaw. Because of his height I had to reach upward. My fist landed above his jaw directly on his front teeth. I felt a sting in my hand as Arthur was staggering back and dropping to his knees.

"My teeth, my teeth," he cried out, holding two of his front teeth in his hand, tears running down his eyes and blood down his face.

I had never seen such a sight. I wanted to drop down to him and say I was sorry. What had I done? I just turned and walked back to Larry, Johnny, and Gerald, and we walked away because I knew that was what they expected me to do.

I was now a tough guy. I had a reputation. Other kids in the neighborhood would fear me. Neither Arthur nor any of his friends would report the incident for fear of retaliation. Ratting about a fight would be the ultimate sin among the boys of Jackson Hill.

Many times in my life I have wondered what happened to Arthur and how he dealt with his two missing teeth. From the time I saw him drop to his knees I knew I had done wrong. In looking back, I suspect

Larry and Johnny stole my bat. They wanted to see a fight and so did my brother, Gerald.

While I was still feeling bad about that one, Larry came up with a break-in plan. "Gonna do our first robbery," is how he put it. "Got some inside help. Johnny's cousin Rex works at Deans Drive Inn. He owes Johnny, and he's gonna leave the basement window unlocked. We go in the basement, up the steps, bust open the cash register, and take money."

"Not doing it, Larry." I was firm. "We could get caught. I don't wanna go to jail."

Larry persisted. He explained to me how he was going to become a professional robber some day. He planned to start with small jobs to learn his trade and move his way up, eventually going for banks. I had already begun to doubt Larry and his pals as viable friends. The B and E idea was over the top.

I made a decision right then to find a way to avoid Larry and his boys and any of their capers. We had already stolen from a fruit market, snuck in a drive-in movie, and I had even distracted a party store owner with a question while Larry and Donnie stole some food right off the store's shelves.

Two days after being confronted with the robbery idea, I got a job weeding celery at a celery farm, a one and a half mile walk away from Uncle Alfred's. I hated the work, but loved the money. After a long week of work, a Friday night movie with Larry and the boys seemed like a good idea. The walk to the movie was three miles. On the way back, I realized we were taking a different route and wasting a lot of time. It was getting late.

As we approached Dean's Drive Inn, closed for the night, Larry informed me of his plan. I tried to talk everybody out of it, Larry, Donnie, and Johnny. They wouldn't listen. Not only wouldn't they listen, I would be considered yellow and lose their friendship if I didn't help.

I was too young and alone too stand up for what I knew was best. I think I realized I would be better off without their friendship, but some how I was having a hard time with the idea of just saying no way, and heading home by myself. All I had to do was stand outside and knock on the window if I saw any sign of trouble. To this day, I have sympathy for young kids who are caught up in circumstances they later regret, seeing trouble clearly but feeling they can't escape from it.

I saw trouble that night clear enough. The police. About fifteen minutes after the boys entered through the basement window I heard a crash inside the building. Donnie had bumped into and knocked over a tray of glass dishes.

I saw a light go on at the house next door to the drive-in. I knocked on an exterior window, and saw Johnny look at me. I gave a motion that signified for them to get out. I decided that I had done enough. As I exited the property into the alley, I looked back and saw a police car turn into the lot. I never stopped running until I reached Uncle Alfred's house.

I was sure the police car had not seen me and I remembered Larry and the boys pledge, "If anyone gets caught, we don't rat on the others. They will grill you for hours, but don't ever give in."

My ma and Uncle Alfred were sleeping, so I quietly went upstairs. This was it, I decided. A close call and the last one. I needed to find new friends.

Unfortunately, it was more than a close call. I can still picture myself, lying on my bed, wringing in sweat, and seeing the red flashing light of the police car pulling into Uncle Alfred's driveway. Some pledge Larry and the boys made, I thought. They hadn't even been grilled for an hour. They must have blurted my name out at the police's first question.

It was a long evening and one of the luckiest of my life. After an hour of tears and the whole truth about my involvement, my life, my ill father, my new friends, and a promise to not ever be seen with them again, I was sent on my way.

A part of me wanted to find Larry and knock a couple of his teeth out, but I was determined to keep my promise to the policeman, as he said, "stay away from that bunch." I spent the whole next morning, a Sunday, lying in bed, wishing I were back on the farm. I missed our family horse, the cows, playing in the barn, and my country friends. I missed Shep and sneaking apples. I even missed the work.

I wondered about my future. I didn't have any friends now. I would have to begin ninth grade in a big strange school. I wondered what I would wear and if I could do the school work. I didn't like my life, but I couldn't give up. I had to find my way. This was a defining hour in my life. I could have given in, joined the bad guys. But, I lived in America. I had a choice. I could feel sorry for myself, resent authority, and look for someone to help me, or I could take responsibility, dig in my heels, and earn my way. My parents were not educated, they had it tough. But, they were proud and loyal Americans.

Ma and Dad didn't have the knowledge to guide me down the right path but what they did have was pride and a love for their country. I don't know what ever happened to Larry, Johnny, and Ron. Thinking back I was so amazed how Larry's mom never talked to Larry about the theft, even though she had to know he stole the Coke.

"God damn cops, always picking on Larry." I can still hear her words while she drank another stolen Coke. She collected welfare, claiming she couldn't work because she had to stay home to take care of her son, Larry.

I never had another conversation with Larry, Johnny and Donnie. They passed by one day when Gerald and I were in the yard lifting weights. Gerald had become obsessed with wanting to build muscles. He had been involved in some neighborhood fights, too, and usually ended up with a black eye.

We watched the three thugs approach and we tensed up, but we were ready for them. They walked closer, and then walked past. They never said a word.

Culture Shock

Just as I started to plan for my return to Aunt Mary's I met a couple new friends, Alex and Bobby. Their vices were different, but these guys weren't much of an improvement over the other three.

They were more interested in girls and finding some alcohol to drink, both new experiences for me. At least, I thought, they're not thieves. Alex and Bobby took me to the roller skating rink where Alex introduced me to Vicki, my first girlfriend. Vicki, a skinny little blonde, invited me to her house. We met at the rink several times and went to movies with Alex and his girlfriend. My new friends convinced me that I should forget about Ravenna, stay in Muskegon, and attend Muskegon Junior High. Their convincing worked and I stayed. Hello Muskegon and Vicki, goodbye Ravenna and Jacqueline Jablonski.

Answers.com defines culture shock as a condition of confusion and anxiety affecting a person suddenly exposed to an alien culture or milieu. As a 15-year-old entering Muskegon Central Junior High as a ninth grader, I faced culture shock. My education from kindergarten through eighth grade was all in one room, with all nine grades under one teacher.

In September of 1956 I entered a junior high school of about 300 kids. My new Jackson Hill friends gave me confidence, and I adjusted. I saved my money to buy new Levis jeans and a Levis jacket and washed them several times so they would be faded. Three buttons undone on my shirt, jacket collar up, Camel cigarettes in my pocket, I was confident.

I could see that I was different; most other boys had crew cuts. I wore my hair long and combed a ducktail in the back. I wasn't concerned about being different because my new friends, Alex and Bobby, were the cool guys. At least, that's what they told me.

So, when the other kids looked at me as though I was weird, I just thought it was because I was special, and a cool dude. And, I had reason to believe that many of the kids who gave me strange looks feared me. I had already been in some fights around town and the word was out that I was trouble. I was a year older than most, physically confident, and a stocky 155 lbs.

The white boys looked the other way when I passed them by. A small group of blacks that hung out together glared at me as if to say, "Hey white boy you want trouble, we will give you trouble." In their view, they were the tough guys.

I had an hour for lunch and I would leave school and hang out by the neighborhood grocery store. It was there that I was introduced to Ike, the leader of a gang called The Pachukas. Ike was recruiting new members. Sizing me up, he asked me to join his gang. He said initiation would be to join him and his friends the next time a fight came up. I told Ike that I might be interested later, but that I was busy with my job and playing football. Joining a gang didn't sound like a wise idea.

The first room I was assigned to was homeroom. I thought this was my class for the day. I chose to sit in the back row as previously advised by Larry. I soon learned that I had five minutes to get to my next class, algebra. I couldn't spell algebra and had no idea what it was. It sounded like some kind of disease.

I turned the wrong way out of homeroom, but was relieved to run into Alex. He told me to go to the end of the hall and turn right. I followed Alex's directions—straight into the girl's gym. Embarrassed, I wandered down several halls before I found my algebra class.

"And you are?" A tall slim teacher wearing glasses pushed down his nose asked me, as I walked into a nearly full classroom.

"Wayne, Wayne Lobdell," I said.

"How about we give you that front seat, Mr. Lobdell? The one close to the door. That will be your assigned seat. We keep that seat for students who can't tell time." The class all laughed.

This was bad. Not only was I being laughed at by thirty kids, but I had to sit in a front seat in a class that I didn't even know what the subject was. I sat in that seat for fifty minutes until the teacher excused the class and asked me to stay. Alone in the room with this person I decided I disliked very much I soon discovered that I was erroneously assigned to an advanced class. I was far from advanced.

I eventually got the picture and found my way to my classes. Although, feeling out of place and not interested in my classes, I only managed to do enough schoolwork to get by with the minimum required to pass. A phys ed teacher talked me into joining the football team. By the time I joined, they had already been practicing for two weeks. I had hardly ever even watched football, let alone played it.

I was new and different, having grown my hair long by then wearing Levis and a Levis jacket. The "jocks' had crew cuts and wore khaki pants. At my second practice, confused about my blocking assignment. I blocked another player from behind. The player, a black kid named Jesse Millwood, challenged me to a fight after practice.

"I'll be there," I said, accepting the challenge.

We agreed to meet behind the gymnasium. I assumed that I didn't have any choice for fear of being called a coward. I had second thoughts when Jesse pulled a switchblade. I should have turned and run. Instead, I took my shirt off and wrapped it around my left hand, thinking I could block the knife with my left and strike him with the other. How stupid can a kid get?

It didn't work very well. Jesse flicked his knife at my wrist. I tried the block and hit plan, but missed with both. I felt a sting and looked at my wrist to see blood. Fortunately, the phys ed teacher came to the scene. The fight was over. Jesse was expelled from school and I was given a lecture.

In retrospect, I should have been expelled as well. The cut on my wrist was long, but not too deep. I still have the scar. I never quite got with it in football. I was as fast and strong as any of them. I just didn't know what I was doing, and didn't feel like I belonged. I quit three days later, but the incident wasn't over yet.

Invitation for Trouble

"Hey white trash, how abouts you and I go outside and rumble?"

I was at the junior high dance with my friend, Alex. Four black teens approached me.

"Why you looking to fight me?" I asked. I had no interest in this encounter.

"You got my friend, Jesse, kicked off the team," said the challenger.

They all gathered around me. I was in trouble, my only salvation being that fighting at the dance would get them kicked out of school. I needed a solution, and the only thing I could think of was Ike and The Pachukas.

"Me and my friends will meet you in the school parking lot tomorrow at noon."

"We will be there man," they all said boldly. At that, they walked away.

In my mind, joining Ike's gang was now a necessity. I assumed Ike was itching for an encounter with the blacks and I was right. He enthusiastically offered to back me in my challenge. Aware of the danger, visualizing clubs, knives and blood, I didn't sleep that night.

I was in a situation that I didn't want to be in, but I came up with an idea before leaving the house the next morning and I made a secret phone call.

As committed, I met Ike and twelve of his friends six blocks from the school parking lot at ten minutes before noon. We walked confidently down the street, and I was side by side with Ike. We were all clad in our Levis attire, shirts unbuttoned in front, dragging our feet along with our white buck shoes.

Ike was a mean looking dude, able to scare most other kids away with a stare alone. With his square jaw and pitted face, he looked much older than the other junior high kids. He was broad shouldered on a 5'11' frame. Just walking beside him made me feel bigger than I was.

All was quiet as we approached the parking lot. In the face of violence, I wondered if my secret idea would work. We looked across the parking lot and spotted what we assumed would be one of our opponents, a young black kid standing on a corner about a half block from the lot. We figured he was there to see if we would show, and to take a head count.

As we waited to see if the rest of our opponents would come foreword, two police cars approached us. I hid my inward sigh of relief. My secret phone call to the police had paid off.

"What are you boys up to?" the officer asked.

"Just out for a walk, sir," our leader, Ike, responded.

"Well, split up and head for home. And do it now."

My nightmare was over. On further invitations to join in a gang fight, I always came up with an excuse.

I often think back at how lucky I was to have evaded that gang fight, as well as how some of the other encounters I was involved in turned out, any one of which could have changed my entire life.

Even though I had a mother and a father who set a good examples for honesty and hard work, I almost lost my way because of my environment and because my parents were not educated enough or aware enough to advise me and guide me. They were good people, but they didn't have a clue about how to prepare my brothers and me for the world we faced.

I don't know what ever happened to Ike and others in his Pachuka gang. I can only guess, and I bet it didn't turn out too good. When I hear and read about youth drugs and crime in the streets across America, I have sympathy for their plight. I wonder how many of them were trapped in an environment that they couldn't see their way out of.

I was fortunate that my dad provided a great example for the value of hard work, and that he and my mother taught me the value of honesty. Yet my dad had a misconception about the dangers of fighting. He, the person who I most looked up to, was genuinely good, but thought fighting was a healthy activity. He saw it as a sport and a matter of pride. He instilled in me the obligation to accept a challenge.

The idea of walking away from a challenge or insult was unthinkable to him. I recall him talking about how strong his father, my grandfather, was. He always looked at men in terms of how strong or tough they were, or who might be able to whip whom.

When this attitude becomes instilled in your brain, your reactions to confrontations and insults becomes automatic. Even as an adult, I have struggled to control that instinct when I have been insulted or threatened. In the few instances that my reactions resulted in physical confrontation, I always wished later that I had found a better solution.

Mikey Monkey Business

My new life in the city was about feeling my way, adjusting to my environment. Often, as I lay alone in bed at night in my bedroom at Uncle Alfred's, I questioned one of my new friends' behavior, yet, I couldn't envision any other path.

Bobby had a secret source for peaches and honey brandy. Our favorite winter entertainment was to share a bottle of brandy to help us keep warm and to become fearless enough to slide behind cars. The sport was only practical on cold nights after a fresh snow and before salt was added to the roads.

The game was to wait at a corner for a car to stop at the stop sign, stomp out our Camel cigarette, slip in behind the car, knees bent and feet together, with our gloved hands grasped onto the back bumper. In this precarious position we'd slide behind the car as it moved away from the corner. The object was to hang on as long as possible before releasing and falling to the side of the road. I held the record for most of the winter until Bobby clung to a slow moving Model A Ford and managed to hang on for a full block and a half.

This was fun, but dangerous. My best excuse for avoiding my friends' activities was to look for work. One week before Christmas of 1956, on the same day that my father was released from the TB sanitarium, I found a job as a pin boy.

Christmas was great that year. My dad, having hoarded the money from the sale of the farm, purchased a two-bedroom ranch style house. A home for him, Ma, and me. Gerald left home to join the Army, and we were proud of him. The only sadness that season was that Lavern had disappeared again.

I tried to concentrate on happy things though, and one of those was my new job. A pin boy sits on the ledge of a concrete pit at the end of each bowling lane, out of sight of the bowlers. His job is to jump into the pit after the pins are knocked down and place the pins into a pin rack, which then automatically resets the pins. A skill is developed to slip two pins into each hand by sliding the pins between the fingers of each hand and then flipping them into the pinsetter—a task that eventually causes swollen knuckles. When the rack is full, the automated pin rack drops downward, positioning the pins on the alley.

At that time, pin boys were paid ten cents a frame. Working one pit on an average night would earn the pin boy about $1 an hour. A few of the more experienced and skilled pin boys would be allowed to handle two lanes, earning as much as $2 an hour on a busy night.

Working in these pits where the pin boys performed provided me the experience of getting to know another set of interesting characters. The most memorable was the kid that fellow workers nick named Mikey Monkey Business. When business was slow, the pin boys had idle time. Drinking, smoking, and occasionally a fist fight could be expected. Then there was always Mike doing monkey business.

One night Mikey asked me to cover his lane while he did some exploring. He was a bony little guy at 5' 5", wore a peach fuzz mustache and walked with a limp. Mikey's exploration involved climbing up to the ceiling above the bowling alleys.

Moving in this area above the alleys amounted to carefully stepping on support beams. A fragile drop ceiling with insulation on it between the beams provided the ceiling above the alleys. Halfway intoxicated on this particular night, Mikey stumbled into the ceiling between the beams. His feet plunged through the ceiling while his two arms clung to the support beams.

What a sight for the alley full of bowlers: two legs hanging down above the alley, insulation hanging down next to him, and a piece of ceiling tile on the bowling lane. Curious amusement shifted to laughter when Mikey's pants caught the edge of the framing and started to fall as he was trying to hoist himself back up, jockey shorts on display. Mikey managed to escape, pants dangling from his feet. He was fired immediately.

The demise of Mikey Monkey Business was my gain. I set doubles for the remainder of that night and thereafter held the pit alley honor of becoming a Doubles Pin boy. I missed Mikey, but not as much as I enjoyed making more than $2 an hour on busy nights.

Escaping the Hood

The bowling alley job kept me busy and away from my trouble making friends. At the close of winter, in the spring of 1957, on my sixteenth birthday, I was able to buy a used motorbike, a "steal of a deal" the seller told me. My dad, who was well enough to work again and had a job as sanitation inspector for the City of Muskegon Heights, said he would rather help me buy a car. For her part, my mother feared the danger of a motorbike. But I was determined to get that "steal of a deal."

The seller told me that I could easily sell it for a profit if I didn't like it. How could I lose? And, my girlfriend Vicki thought I looked cool on that motorbike.

Joining the track team, where I competed with moderate success in the hundred-yard dash, hurdles, and shot put, enabled me to get away from questionable friends and meet some of the school athletes. One of the benefits, although not that significant to me at the time, was that I had to study some to maintain the C grades to stay on the team. My only motivation to do anything in school was to have grades minimally sufficient to stay eligible to compete.

Once I involved myself in sports, I began to distance myself from Alex and Bobby. Football, basketball, and baseball star, Jim Erickson, became my new friend. The friendship began after I gave Jim a ride home from school on my motorbike. The friendship got better though when I let him ride it.

Jim and I had a favorite game that we'd play when I visited him at his house. We would bet a dime on who could walk the farthest on his hands. Farm boy that I was, I had not learned to throw a football or shoot a basketball like Jim, but I was a regular winner in the hand walking competition. Jim, a quarterback, saw my coordination and was convinced that he would be handing off the ball to me when we entered football for 10th grade in the fall.

That friendship turned out to be a good one, but what it was first based on, the motorbike, didn't turn out so well. It was in the repair shop more than I rode it. I sold it for half of what I paid for it; no steal of a deal after all.

After a month without transportation, my dad helped me buy a 1949 Ford straight stick. Now, I was a real hot dog. I soon learned to "peel in all three gears," the process of squealing tires on the pavement as you accelerate on shifting gears.

Although Jim had become my new friend away from school and liked my having a car, he was a little cautious about being around me at school activities. I continued to wear my hair long, only slightly toning down my ducktail style hair cut. I first sensed that Jim might have been somewhat uncomfortable with our friendship at a junior high dance when I came over to stand next to him while he was with some of the other athletes. It was a Friday night dance at the school gymnasium. The disc jockey, the kid putting on the records and naming the songs over the PA, was Jim Bakker. And yes, I do mean the Jim Bakker who later became famous with his wife Tammy Faye.

The boys were on one side of the room and girls on the other. On the dance floor it was mostly girls dancing with girls. Feeling a need too say something or make some type of move to fit in, I asked Jim, "Who is that blonde standing over there? The one standing next to the cheerleader?"

"The blonde is Cherri Collinge, president of our class. The cheerleader next to her is her twin sister, Terry."

Then Jim looked at me with a grin and said, "Why don't you ask one of them to dance?"

I was probably one of a few kids in junior high who didn't know who the cute Collinge twins were. Cherri, the outgoing and flirty one and Terry, the pretty all American girl athlete with a ponytail. But given the group of friends that I had been hanging out with, I knew very little about the Collinge twins.

Jim's suggestion was more like a dare and I liked dares. Even though Terry seemed to be more my type, I could see that she was the ideal class example of perfection, in both academics and activities, and way out of my league. I would not feel comfortable even attempting to talk to her.

Not that I didn't have self-confidence; I was now hanging out with the school jocks. Rather, I just had the feeling that Terry was too prim and proper. She seemed to have a different set of values than I did. How I knew all this from just a look, I'm not sure but I had the same apprehensions at the dance as I did about talking to Jacqueline Jablonski when I was at Hoogstraat.

Yet, I still felt the need to accept Jim's challenge. Cherri looked our way and smiled. Taking the smile as a signal, I made my move. I decided to ask Cherri to dance and I walked across the room in her direction. On the way, I started to have second thoughts. What if she laughed at me? If she said no, I would just have to turn my heels and walk away, and be embarrassed in the eyes of all my new friends. I asked her anyway.

"Sure, I would like to dance with you," she responded with a smile. I should have been thrilled but I had another concern. My very limited dancing skills. Plus, my tongue was tied in double knots. What do I say? What do I talk about?

She made it easy. Both the dancing and the conversation. As I recall, Cherri took the lead. It was a slow dance and I didn't press too close as Cherri was rather busty for a junior high girl. I just followed along, sliding my feet to a two-step. Cherri did most of the talking and as the dance ended we were still talking and continued to another dance.

I didn't realize that one dance is being polite whereas two dances is making a move. Glancing out of the corner of my eye, I noted that Cherri's twin seemed to be giving her the evil eye. We mostly talked about what classes we were taking and which teachers we liked best. At the end of the second dance I thanked Cherri and walked back to my friends.

Jim and his buddies made some wise cracks about my pressing too close to Cherri. At that point I began to sense this entirely different social circle that I was flirting with. I begin to wonder if I would fit in.

I am not sure if it happened accidentally or if I subconsciously plotted it that way, but as the dance activity ended I stayed behind a few minutes as my friends exited the building. As I moved toward the exit, I found myself walking down the stairs next to Cherri. I just kept walking next to her as she was talking and asking me questions. As we proceeded away from the building, I said, " I guess I will go this way home and walk with you."

"So, you're walking me home?" she asked.

"Yeah, I can go this way," I said. Cherri just smiled at me and we walked on to her house. We ran out of things to talk about pretty quickly but fortunately her home on Leahy Street was only a few blocks away. When we arrived her twin sister, Terry, was waiting on the porch and she didn't look too happy. I said goodbye and was quickly on my way.

Cherri's twin, Terry, whose relationship with her twin was more like that of a big sister, met Cherri with a lecture about being seen walking home with a "hoodlum."

Cherri and Terry had four older sisters, two older brothers, and a younger sister. They lived near the school and their mom, Trudy, was often a parent chaperone at school events. In addition to being class president, Cherri played the violin. Terry was a cheerleader, played the piano and was the school's best girl athlete. They were both A students, but Terry was National Honor Society material. Cherri flirted with and dated boys and was often disorganized and forgetful. Terry, more cautious and shy with boys, was all business and looked after Cherri.

Wayne 'the hood' in 1957.

Wayne 'the hood' on his cycle in 1957.

Seeing the Light

A Magic Moment

My next Collinge twin encounter came two days later. I crossed paths with Terry as I left homeroom to go to my first class. Surprise! Terry smiled and said "Hi."

I don't think I ever recall a "Hi" having more significance to me. For some reason my heart just jumped. I didn't know why, it just happened, and for the next two weeks I looked to spot Terry between classes.

On one other occasion she again smiled at me and said hello. I also noticed Cherri between classes, and she was friendly and spoke to me as well, but I couldn't seem to comprehend why seeing Terry caused a unique feeling for me.

I began thinking about Terry while sitting in class and again at home at night. I had wandering thoughts about Terry. I daydreamed about talking to her, imagined what I would say. Then, I would remind myself that Terry was 14 and I was 16 and that Terry was in a different social world than I was.

Coincidentally, Vicki had been randomly assigned as Terry's Home Economics partner. She sported pierced earrings, a 'no no' for girls in the fifties, and proudly showed off a photo of her 'cool' boyfriend, me, on a motor cycle.

I soon began to realize that my feelings for Vicki were not for real, not if I was thinking more about a girl who I was yet to even talk to beyond that single word. A notice for the next junior high dance caught my eye and my imagination. Should I go? If I did go, would I dare to try to talk to Terry?

I went and I did. Making my move was not easy. I stood for close to an hour on the boys' side of the room, with Jim and two other new friends, Tom and Brian. As I stood there, trying not to be obvious with my interest, I couldn't help but notice that Tommy Sheridan, a boy I had seen Terry walking with between classes, danced with her two times in a row. It's now or never, I decided, as I noticed Terry standing alone when the next song, a slow one, began.

"Would you like to dance?" I asked her. I was prepared for a rejection, but to my surprise, I got a simple "Sure" and even a smile.

The transition from nervous to fun was amazing. I quickly felt at ease, comfortable, like I belonged. Terry, even at the young age of 14, had a magic of making people feel comfortable. Terry asked me where I lived, asked about my family, and how I happened to move to Muskegon. I told her about my school at Hoogstraat and how I found junior high classes to be a strange and new experience. After a couple of slow dances, a fast tune was played. I excused myself with the admission that I didn't know how to fast dance, but not before I asked her another question.

"I go your way when I go home, can I walk with you?" The words came out awkwardly. Her "yes" was a thrill. And that is how it all began.

As I began showing more and more interest in seeing Terry again, she made some hints about my hairstyle and attire. I took the hint quickly, trimming my hair and changed from jeans to khakis. These changes were genuine on my part, but didn't satisfy everyone.

Terry dating me became an issue at Central Junior High. Other students, teachers, and Terry's family all had talks with her about dating me. It just didn't seem right, they told her. Terry seemed destined for a great future and I was somewhat of a hoodlum with a bad reputation. Although I had distanced myself from the gang kids and changed my look, my behavior was still suspect. I still skipped classes, disregarded my homework, and even engaged in a few fist fights.

In one of my gym classes, I took a smack in the face during a basketball scrimmage from Eddie Brinkley. The smack was an accident, but he laughed about it. I didn't think my puffed lip was funny. A little "sorry about that" would have done the trick.

After class, outside the gym, I approached Eddie to tell him that he owed me an apology. Eddie disagreed. "Shove it," he told me, and he said it in the presence of others. In my way of thinking, I had no option.

I gave Eddie a shove. Eddie doubled up his fist and took a swing.

The fight began. After a few blows, we began to wrestle and I ended up on top. Students gathered around and watched for several minutes before the gym teacher came out to break up the fight. Terry's older sister, Janice, saw it all and expressed disgust with my behavior. Eddie accepted responsibility for starting the fight, neither of us was punished, but I received several verbal lectures and criticism from other students and teachers.

I don't remember that Terry ever said anything to me. I am sure others said much to her, but she apparently never wanted to accept those criticisms of me. I am not sure I understood why she stuck by me, given my behavior. She just did. Somehow, Terry apparently felt that I would grow up. I did, but it took a while. Thank heaven for her patience.

I didn't realize it at the time, but I had narrowly escaped a dangerous path. I could have joined The Pachuka gang. I could have stuck with Larry, who thought the best way to make money was to steal it. I could have been run over by a car while hanging onto bumpers on Marquette Avenue. I could have been knifed or shot. My original Muskegon friends all said that I had ditched them to become "High Sci," as in high society.

I was a long ways from high society, and I knew it. My new friends, except for Terry, were not angels. We still went for the booze, and were always ready for a fight. A pecking order of who could kick whose butt was still important in my new group's standings. The only difference was beer instead of cheap brandy or wine, and fighting was done with fists, not knives.

Terry though was my little angel. We agreed to start going steady on May 14th of 1957. This was not a popular move in the eyes of Terry's family or the many teachers who held Terry in such high esteem. She had a different vision of me than others did, though. She transformed me, but did it in a subtle way. She apparently saw qualities in me that even I didn't see in myself. On the occasions when she could get me to do some homework, she found that I could do the work easily whenever I had the motivation to do so. I just rarely had the motivation and I hardly ever even brought my schoolwork home. I wasn't looking into the future, only at attaining passing grades. Plus, I didn't have time to study. I had jobs.

Making the Sale

My work responsibilities expanded in the summer of 1957. My boss, Mr. Patterson, decided that he needed more workers like me. So, when he interviewed applicants for the summer season, he had them talk with me. And I knew what to look for – country boys. I knew that my friends wouldn't be good workers; I wanted the kid who had chores to do at home.

Once hired, I tried to find ways to keep the new workers motivated. I was having my first try at leadership. Although not realizing at the time, between this experience at the fruit market and my dad's advice to "do more than expected," I was, at a young age, developing the work skills that would pay big dividends later.

"I can show you how to make more money than that fruit market job," Lavern told me and my two cousins, Leo and Roma.

My big brother was home on one of his surprise visits. This time claiming to be a manager for a publication distribution company. He sounded convincing when he explained how easy it was to sell $200 in subscriptions and earn $20 in commission for one day's work. A two-hour Saturday morning training session and we were off to seek the riches of selling magazines.

"A few little harmless fibs," he said we had to tell. "People like to feel they are helping you, so tell them what they want to hear. You are in a scholarship contest to earn money for college. You tell them that three winners will be named with first place getting the biggest scholarship," he said enthusiastically. "Be specific to make it believable. You're in third place now and a few more sales and you could be challenging the lead."

He went on to offer more ideas like these, such as offering to come back someday and wash their windows, mow their lawn, or wash their car. Leo and I knew Lavern well enough to have our doubts, but were willing to give it a try. Roma was an all A student who liked to memorize poetry, but she was a little naïve.

"Will you bring me back to wash the windows?" she asked Lavern.

"No, no, no," he told her. "They are not going to expect you to wash their windows. You're just saying that to be nice."

"How much will the scholarship be?" Roma wondered aloud.

Leo and I laughed and Lavern threw up his hands and rolled his eyes.

"You're not getting a scholarship. You're just saying that so they will want to buy the magazines to help you." Roma still looked a little confused.

I had my spiel all memorized and Lavern assigned me a block to work. "I'm giving you the best block." He said. "I can just tell by the looks of the homes. You're going to sell $100 in the next two hours." He added a "Go get 'em" as he left me to make his other assignments.

"So, how much did you sell," my brother asked, an hour and half later after I'd finished my block. "Did you make the $100 goal?"

"Nope," I responded

"Fifty, twenty-five, how much?" he pleaded.

"How about zero?" I said.

He looked down the street, squinting his eyes. "Look, that house over there with the nice little old couple sitting on the porch. How could you not sell them?"

"They said they didn't read magazines," I explained.

"But they have kids or grandkids, I'm sure." With that he added, "Come with me."

We headed for the house with the little old couple sitting on the porch. I was embarrassed to go back to the house because they had already refused me. As we approached, Lavern pointed to the mailbox. The letters on the box said Albert Granger.

"Excuse me," he said, "are you the Grangers?"

"Yes, what can I do for you?" The lady had come to the door.

"Albert Granger?"

"Yes, that's my husband over there," the lady said, pointing to the man on the porch.

"Wow, what a coincidence. I came back over here with my brother when he told me he thought your last name was Granger. We are related to the Grangers in Chicago, second or third cousins I think."

That line of nonsense he just made up at the spur of the moment got us in the door. In the next ten minutes Lavern went through the whole scholarship spiel, offering to wash windows and so on. When they said they didn't read magazines, he just asked, "Do you have grandchildren."

"We have an eighteen year old grandson."

"Do you think your grandson would read Sports Illustrated if it was given to him?

"Well, I suppose he would," said Albert.

"Wow, look here I have a special on Sports Illustrated. And my little brother here will get 10 points in the scholarship contest. You're so nice to do this for him." Lavern started writing up the order.

In a period of fifteen minutes, with the use of several other sales gimmicks, he ended up selling the Grangers two other subscriptions. Before he left, he had information on the lady next door and went to that house saying we were sent there by the Grangers, "because they knew you would want to help us out." The neighbor lady reluctantly bought one subscription.

I got the point, but knew I couldn't do what he had just done. Next we picked up Leo. He had sold one small order. But, where was Roma? We couldn't find her. We looked up and down the street she was assigned to, and the next street over, too. No Roma. We were becoming concerned. Then we spotted her. We all cracked up laughing. Roma was on a ladder washing windows. She didn't get it and, for that matter, neither did I. This was the first and only job failure of my life.

Three days after my retirement from magazine sales, the police came to our house looking for Lavern. He was in violation, the policeman told my dad, for soliciting magazines without registering. They didn't locate Lavern because he didn't come home. He disappeared again for eighteen months.

One-Foot Driver

My quarterback friend Jim's plan of me being his running back on the JV football team lasted about as long as my magazine sales career. I broke my leg in practice before the first game.

I incurred the injury while scrimmaging as a JV second stringer, against the varsity team. One of the varsity players clipped me from behind. I learned why clipping is a fifteen-yard penalty in football.

I sat out the rest of that practice in pain. Afterwards, I dragged myself to the athletic director's office. His name was Harry Potter, an ex-military man.

"Tough it out boy," he told me. "Go home. Put a little ice on it. You'll be ready for practice tomorrow."

I never slept that night. The pain in my knee was excruciating. I returned to school the next day, but feared returning to Mr. Potter's office. My problem came to a head when the school nurse spotted me dragging my leg, grimacing in pain, as I walked down the hallway. She took me to the hospital where x- rays showed a severely torn ligament in my right knee. A cast was placed from my ankle to the top of my leg, to be worn for two months. My football season was over; so was my fruit market and pin boy jobs.

I had two problems with my crutches. The first was driving a straight stick car with only my left leg functioning. Fortunately, my 1949 Ford had a throttle, a lever on the dashboard which served as an accelerator. I simply hoisted my right leg across the front seat from my position behind the wheel, started the car in neutral, put the clutch in with my left foot, put her in first gear, and then slowly released the clutch at the same time I slowly accelerated with the throttle.

To change gears, I just pushed the clutch in, shifted the gear, and returned my hand to the throttle. This was a rather dangerous driving procedure, but my friends laughed about it and my parents didn't have a clue.

My second problem with crutches was carrying books to all my classes. Guess who toted my books from class to class for me? Terry, amidst teasing from friends and teachers. She dashed back and forth through the halls to make sure I had my books, and still made it to her classes on time. Even today, I still can't believe she did that for me.

I had lost my pin boy job, but once I got out of my cast, I found that I could make more money shoveling snow out of driveways than I could setting pins. The snow shoveling game involved heading for the wealthy homes in North Muskegon immediately after a heavy snow. Shovel in my trunk, I would knock on doors.

"Would you like your drive shoveled out?" I'd ask whoever answered the door.

"How much do you charge?' they'd usually ask me.

"What ever you think it is worth," I'd say.

I could do the average job in less than an hour. The homeowner would estimate the time and generously pay me $2 to $3. Early on I developed a plan to maximize my profits. The first time I did a job I worked at a steady, but a rapid pace, enabling the homeowner to establish a price off the time I spent. The next time I returned, I would go to work on the drive without knocking on the door, assuming they would want the job done. They usually didn't know when I started and, even though I worked faster to get the job done in half the time, I was paid the same amount. My price had been established.

On a fresh snow day I could make $20 to $25 – a week's wages at the bowling alley. I often called in sick for school when a good snow day came. On more than one occasion, after missing a day of school, Terry called me to come to her house to prepare me for one of my exams; all part of her way to help me in school and encourage me, while never criticizing me for my behavior she didn't always agree with. To Terry, a day of school was more important than any amount of money.

The Pugilist

The two most famous local professional sports heroes in Muskegon in the 1950's were All-American quarterback, Earl Morrall, and a world's lightweight boxing contender named Kenny Lane. Morrall went on to become an NFL MVP in Baltimore and quarterbacked the Super Bowl Champion Miami Dolphins to the only undefeated season ever in the NFL. Kenny Lane maintained Muskegon as his hometown and lost close decisions for the World's Lightweight Championship on three occasions. Both men were my heroes.

Kenny trained in a makeshift boxing gym above a bar in Muskegon Heights. The workout facility was sponsored by the Catholic Youth Organization (CYO). The CYO boxing team was exceptionally talented, largely because of the influence of Kenny Lane and his manager, Pete Petoskey. Team members included future featherweight Olympians Oscar German, and welterweight Phil Baldwin. They were both members of the 1960 Olympic boxing team with teammate Cassius Marcellus Clay, later to become Muhammad Ali. Another CYO team member was state middleweight champion, Solomon Fox. My dad, while working his job in Muskegon Heights, had actually met Solomon Fox in person.

On a snowy January evening in 1958, Dad asked me to bring my gym shorts and tennis shoes and to come with him. I didn't know where we were going. "It's a surprise," he said. A surprise it was.

Dad brought me to the CYO boxing gym. We walked up a narrow flight of stairs to the space used as the gym. It was over an old corner saloon on a side street near downtown Muskegon Heights. Entering the gym, I could hear the sound of punching bags and smell the sweat in the air. I was pleased to see Kenny Lane sparring in the ring with Phil Baldwin, but began to wonder why my Dad had me bring my gym shorts. I soon found out.

"Right this way," Pete Petoskey pointed me in the direction of the locker room after my Dad introduced me to both him and Solomon Fox. What is going on? What am I doing here? I had been gaining confidence in my fighting skills and my dad had heard about some of my neighborhood tussles, but this environment was out of my class. What was I to do though? I certainly couldn't refuse.

I had not been beaten in a fist fight or wrestling match since my cousin Leo punched me in the nose when I was twelve. I prepared myself mentally to find out what losing was about.

I was speechless and my heart was beating as I came out of the locker room to have the trainer, Mel Burns, place headgear over my head and lace up my gloves. My immediate reaction was to take note that the headgear didn't provide much protection. As Burns led me to the corner of the ring I noticed that my opponent was going to be none other than middleweight, Solomon Fox.

Although only three inches taller and ten pounds heavier than me, he seemed to be twice my size. Just as I was about to say this isn't fair, Burns put a mouthpiece in my mouth. Gee, at least I may still have my teeth when this is over, I thought.

Every muscle in my body was tight. I held my hands in front of me and danced around Fox like I was Sugar Ray Robinson, wondering when Fox was going to lash out and take my head off. Fox held his hands low and didn't throw a punch. After about thirty seconds, which seemed more like thirty minutes, Burns came into the ring to tell me that the object was for me to throw punches. "And, by the way," he said, "Solomon will not be hitting you."

Inside, I gasped a sigh of relief. Now I got it; the object was to see how I could throw punches while Fox practiced his defense. But, what if I hit him and he doesn't like it. What if he doesn't like the plan?

I didn't want to disappoint my dad though, who I assumed had over-estimated my potential and set this match up. I threw punches at Solomon for two rounds, having difficulty holding my hands up after about two minutes into the three-minute timed rounds. Solomon just ducked, bobbed, and weaved, and slipped all my punches. Seemed like a funny way to begin my boxing career— neither of us landed a punch.

On my next training session I got to spar with Kenny Lane. If Fox could be described as elusive, Kenny was like invisible. I would see an opening and throw a punch, only to have it miss him by an inch or more. The difference between pros and amateurs is that amateurs duck punches whereas pros slip punches, causing the punch to closely slip by the target—allowing the pro to be in position to counter punch. Fortunately for me, Kenny didn't counter punch against me.

After one week of lessons and sparring, I was informed that a box-off would be held between me and two others to determine who would become the CYO welterweight novice competitor in Grand Rapids Golden Gloves. I felt my boxing career was moving a little too fast, and suggested that I wait another year. That, the men informed me, wasn't the plan. At the insistence of my dad and Pete Petoskey, I agreed to proceed.

My first competitor was a tall, long-armed kid called Freddy. Freddy should have been a dancer, instead of a boxer. I chased him around the ring for three rounds and was awarded the win, mainly because he didn't do much of anything offensively. At 5'7" and just over 150 lbs, with a slim waist and the upper body of a body builder, I apparently seemed intimidating to lanky Freddy.

My next opponent was Elmer, a wild swinger, about the same weight and height as me. The first round was close, but I knocked him down in the second with a left hook, and staggered him a couple times in the third. I won the decision and was on my way to the Grand Rapids Golden Gloves a week later.

My fist opponent in the Golden Gloves was disqualified for weighing in over the 147-pound welterweight limit. In thinking back, I should have eaten about four hamburgers to also get disqualified and get out of this fix I was in. Instead, I skipped breakfast and lunch to just make weight. I felt weak when the time came to fight. I also felt intimidated entering a ring before 3,000 spectators at the Grand Rapids Civic Center.

After my first look at my opponent though, Doug McLeod, I felt quite confident. He just didn't look that tough. Fifteen seconds into the first round, I had a different feeling. I sensed trouble. When I came charging after him with left jabs and straight rights, he didn't duck, he just slipped my punches.

McLeod moved around the ring smoothly, more like Kenny Lane than the novices I had faced in the box off. Suddenly, near the end of the first round I felt like a bowing ball had just hit me in the stomach. And, I never saw it coming. The bell rang and I staggered to my corner, gasping for air. I gagged as smelling salts were placed under my nose to help me recover.

Seems like I hardly got seated in the corner and the bell rang for round two. Before I left the corner, Kenny Lane said to me, "Go out there swinging. He can't hit you if he's being hit. Be first. Be first." I was desperate, and had no other choice but to take Kenny's advice. My first punch and the second landed on the side of McLeod's face. Keep swinging, be first, and be first.

I was keeping him on the defensive, but never catching him with a solid punch. Just as my arms started to feel heavy that damn invisible bowling ball hit me in the stomach again. Instantly, as I dropped my arms in reaction, I felt like I was hit with a baseball bat square on the jaw. The next thing I remember was," Seven, eight, nine."

I struggled to get to my feet. The merciful referee stopped the fight, calling a TKO win for McLeod. McLeod, trained by his professional boxing father, went on to win the state championship. He won the remainder of his fights by KO. He later reached the quarterfinals of the National Golden Gloves and then had a successful professional career.

Terry had come to watch the fight with my parents but she never saw a thing. She told me later that she looked at the floor until the fight was over. As for my Dad, I think he figured out from that fight that despite pulling the only strings he had and keeping his fingers crossed, his son was not going to be the next Rocky Marciano.

Wayne and Terry dating, 1959

Wayne in Golden Gloves, 1958

One More Time

I continued to train, not wanting to go out a loser. My involvement in boxing enhanced my reputation among my friends – at least in those who thought being a tough guy was important. On nights out on the town with friends, after a few drinks, looking for a fight seemed to be a popular idea for excitement.

On a Saturday night at one of the teen dances we liked to go to, my friends Brain and Mike and I were becoming a little noisy in the corner of the room.

"Hey, why don't you guys shut to f—k up!" said a tough-looking guy wearing a tight shirt to show off his muscular body. We told him to bug off. He wasn't intimidated.

"Which one of you boys wants to step outside with me?" he retorted back.

My friends looked at me. By this time I was getting pretty good at sizing up competition and I didn't really want to fight this guy. My philosophy: When in doubt, find a way out – delay and maybe the problem will go away.

"I'll go outside with you," I said, "but not tonight." I gave him a confident look and then added, "they have police out there this time of night. I will meet you in the parking lot next Saturday at 7 o'clock." He accepted my offer and my friends assured me they would be there in case he brought friends.

My Monday night workout at the CYO included a sparring session with Kenny Lane; one of those defensive workouts for Kenny where I get to swing away and not get hit in return. Just as I entered the ring with Kenny, this guy I have scheduled a parking lot fight with walked in. I leaned against the ropes and glared at him and he looked shocked. He probably thought at that point that he had a date to fight Kenny Lane's sparring partner. For my part, I did nothing to dissuade him of this notion. I moved around the ring, flexing my muscles. When I looked back he was gone. He didn't show in the parking lot that Saturday night and I was mighty happy about it. I figured if he had showed, with disregard for my sparring with Kenny Lane, I would have been in deep trouble.

I agreed to one more boxing match. The annual Hart Fair, held every July in Hart, Michigan, planned a boxing show, featuring amateur boxers from Muskegon against boxers from Grand Rapids. Before a crowd of about 2,000, I was in the fourth fight of the evening in a match against another novice, Jimmy Manning.

The first three fights had featured rather lackluster exhibition matches between high ranked amateurs. The crowd was getting bored watching cautious boxing matches and was ready for some action. They got their wish. To add to the flavor of the event, Manning was black. Back then, black vs. white always made for a little more excitement in a boxing match.

I can't recall how it came about, but one of my friends, Tom Perry, decided I should have the nickname "Snapper." As the bell rang, Tom yelled out, " Go get 'em Snapper!" Then another friend yelled, "Go Snapper!"

Fired up, I tore into Manning like a bull at the sound of the bell. Manning swung back. One of his punches caught me on the chin, knocking me off balance and causing me to stumble to the canvas. I was up quickly and we kept slugging it out. The crowd loved seeing two novices going toe to toe. With Kenny Lane in my corner, I was the local favorite and soon the whole crowd was yelling "Snapper, Snapper."

Our fight went three rounds. I decked Manning once in the second and staggered him in the third. I was awarded the win by split decision. Again, Terry never saw the fight. She just looked at the floor.

I was never so exhausted in my life as I was after that fight. I went straight to the locker room and vomited. I also made a decision. The Hart Fair was the end of my boxing career. Well, at least it was the end of planned boxing matches. At home, sometimes they happened on the spur of the moment.

My Dad still kept two pair of boxing gloves in the basement. He never lost his interest in watching a good fight, be it with his kids or an adult boxing match. On the night I am thinking of, Gerald had just taken Leo and then me down in arm wrestling matches. Gerald had been released from the army because of his reading handicap and Leo was home on leave from the Army. At Dad's smiling suggestion, we next went to the basement with the boxing gloves.

The first match was Gerald and me. As I put on the gloves, I remembered all the punches I had taken from Gerald while growing up. Our match lasted about 20 seconds with Gerald on the seat of his pants. Next came Leo. I looked at Leo while my Dad laced up his gloves.

"Hey Leo, I'm remembering that punch in the nose when I was twelve."

Leo took a look back at me and calmly slipped off the gloves.

"No way, I've seen enough," he said.

Leo's decision was fine with me. I had mixed emotions about knocking Gerald to the floor, some feelings about sought-after revenge but yet also not feeling all that good about humiliating him.

My other revenge came a year later when Lavern bolted into the house one day. He had been drinking, was loud, swearing, and arguing with my dad. I told him to shut up. He didn't. I wrestled him to the floor, convincing him that I was in charge now.

One other encounter is worthy of mention, for the sake of my dad. I was downtown with Dad one day when he and another driver accidentally backed into each other while backing out of opposite parking spaces. The other driver, a husky young man who looked to be in his late twenties, bounded from his car, obviously angry. While I was still in the passenger seat of my dad's car, the man gave my Dad a shove.

Frail from never totally recovering from his illness, my dad staggered back as the man shoved him. Realizing that a confrontation was evolving, I bolted from the car. Approaching the scene of my dad and this other angry man, I quickly made a personalized observation. My dad, this proud man, once known to be "tougher than nails," actually was now physically unable to defend himself. He stood there trembling, ready to use what strength he had left in his body to try to defend himself against this thoughtless bully. I can never remember, in all my life's encounters, being more enraged at what I saw.

The man saw me coming but he didn't have a second to defend himself. I unleashed a right hand punch square on his jaw. I could feel the jolt from his jaw through my entire arm. His eyes rolled shut and he collapsed backward against his car, slumping to the pavement.

For a minute I was concerned about how badly I had injured him. He managed to rise to his feet slowly though, dazed and confused. He apologized, returned to his car, and drove away.

My dad, now calm and smiling, gave me a hug. His son never became a Rocky Marciano, but that confrontation was a special moment. In future years, as Dad proudly described this incident to others, that other driver became a little larger and hit the deck a little harder each time he told the story.

"Have Yourself Some Dinner"

Though my dad hadn't regained all his strength since recovering from TB, his Muskegon Heights job still paid quite well and he continued to work hard. He took on additional part time jobs and saved enough money to buy some Consumers Power Utility stock. The stock did well, enabling him to buy a new car for the first time. He also helped me buy a 1955 Oldsmobile.

I was in seventh heaven with that car, a hardtop, silver with red interior. I added bubble skirts, waxed it so shiny you could use it as mirror. I added decals and washed it nearly every day. Recalling the ticket I got for speeding, for doing over 100 miles an hour, shows that at this time, despite every life lesson I'd learned, I was still a bit immature.

I can hardly recall a time when my father was home, whether he was sick or healthy, when we didn't have an extra mouth to feed, regardless of how tight we were for money; from Grandpa DeWilder to Uncle Alfred to Patricia the foster girl, cousins visiting the farm, or whoever stopped by. I recall the most frequent visitor at dinner time at our house in Muskegon to be cousin Leo.

Leo's mom and dad had kicked him out of the house, so he just stayed wherever he could find a bed. Frequently, at dinner time, Leo would conveniently come by our home and say, "Just thought I'd stop by," while sizing up the dinner table. My dad would always say, "Pull up a chair and have yourself something to eat."

On Leo's twenty-first birthday he inherited some money from his deceased father, a few thousand dollars I would guess. No more "just stopping by" for Leo." This was not lost on my dad. "Now that Leo's got some money," he said, "he forgot about us. Just wait until Leo runs out of money and comes over here at dinner time. I will just send him on his way."

Sure enough, three months later, word was out that party time was over for Leo. He was broke again. One evening, here came Leo walking up our driveway at dinner time. We were all prepared for my dad to let off some steam and send our ungrateful cousin on his way.

"Just thought I'd stop by," said Leo as he sized up a bowl of meatballs and spaghetti Ma had just set out on the kitchen table.

Ma smiled to herself and she, Gerald, and I were ready for Dad's attack. He rose from his seat, took one look at Leo's hungry face and just said, "Well sit down here and have yourself some of my spaghetti."

Moving On

Analyzing Lavern

Throughout high school, my brother Lavern continued to disappear for months at a time and then suddenly reappear, usually in need of money. His alcoholism and disorderly behavior would frequently embarrass me and others in our family when news clips about his misdeeds appeared in the Muskegon Chronicle.

His chronically bad behavior resulted in local jail and even state prison sentences. My dad paid many of the fines and he and my mother shed many tears over Lavern's problems. A psychiatric analysis of Lavern paid for by my dad, resulted in a conclusion that Lavern had a very high IQ, but had a personality disorder that couldn't likely ever be fixed.

On the surprise occasions that my brother Lavern came home he would always do so with the commitment that he had changed. He was "on a path to a better life," he promised. Ma always believed him, even if no one else could.

"Lavern is doing better now," she'd say. "He has changed his ways. He is going to get a job. He's going to stop drinking." Time after time, the same routine, but she never gave up on him.

At Ma's urging, my dad would help him find a job. A few days later he would be in jail for disorderly conduct, having become intoxicated and arrested for some type of disruptive behavior, or for cashing bad checks. He would open a bank account and just keep cashing checks until he was arrested. He was eventually sent to Jackson Prison for a year as a chronic offender. He didn't commit serious crimes, just a lot of little ones; disturbing the peace, overdrawing his account with small checks.

Making the Grade

The rest of my high school years went by fast. Terry and I continued to date and I continued to keep busy shoveling snow in the winter and taking care of lawns in the summer. Jobs to pay for cars to drive were more important to me than participating in sports or being concerned about school grades.

Before entering my senior year, Terry and I started talking about our futures. My idea was to join the Marines and advance my education while experiencing the excitement of being in the military. Terry talked me into considering college. The only problem with this plan was my grades. So, for the first time, and with Terry's help and encouragement, I decided to do my homework as a senior. I started to enjoy my classes and made the honor roll.

Our relationship did have one interruption. One Saturday, while working at trimming some shrubs for my favorite employer, Mrs. Golden, in North Muskegon, a couple of friendly girls walked by. I recognized them as high school tennis stars, Ann Hathaway from Muskegon and Nancy Foote from North Muskegon. We chatted. They came by the next Saturday to the chagrin of Mrs. Golden.

My acquaintance and a few dates with Ann led to a decision that Terry and I should date others for awhile. It was a short while. Terry and I were back together a couple months later, forever.

Thanks to Terry I decided to go to college. Still, given my modest cumulative high school grade point average, choices were limited for me. With some help from my parents and weekend jobs, I was able to attend Ferris State College in Big Rapids, a hundred miles from home.

Terry attended Muskegon Community College on an academic scholarship. I drove those one hundred miles home every other weekend to see Terry. As for activities, I made the Ferris Bulldog football team and quit after very little game time after having a re-occurrence of my knee injury. I worked on the school newspaper and ran the 400 meters on the track team.

That first summer, my cousin Leo and I went to Chicago to look for work. We had heard about the good wages some factory workers made, and we wanted in. My Uncle Charlie lived in one of Chicago's many mixed neighborhoods in the south side and he let us stay with him. Every morning Leo and I would get up early and head out on our job search. After a week of this with nothing to show for it, we were about to give up. Then, we spotted a help-wanted ad that said a paper box company was hiring. We high-tailed it down to the company, stood in line for hours, and were finally given a written test and told that we would receive a call the next day if we were going to be offered a job. I got the call. Leo didn't. He went back to Muskegon.

I felt bad for Leo, as well as a kid by the name of Phillip who lived next door. He was about my age, a nice kid and we talked occasionally. He lived with his family and two other families in one house. After coming home to Uncle Charlie's after my first day on the job, Philip asked me if the box company hired "colored." My observations of my work place and the test that was irrelevant to the job made my answer obvious. I gave Phillip a sympathetic response, "I don't think they do." I thought about the unfairness of it. I had come to his neighborhood from out of town and got a job that he would loved to have, and was perfectly capable of doing; yet, I still recognized the situation as just the way things were at the time.

Coincidentally, that summer Barack Obama was born in Honolulu, Hawaii on August 4, 1961. Who could have imagined in those days that a brilliant young American of partial African descent would someday come to Chicago and become President of the United States. I hope Phillip is proud, wherever he is. Sometimes good things take a long time to happen in America, but we eventually get it right.

My job was not fun and Uncle Charlie was no ball of laughs, either, but one weekend I had a fabulous four-day surprise. My parents came to visit me and brought Terry with them. I had looked forward to Terry's daily letters and wrote to her as well. Seeing her in person was a thrill. We all crowded into Uncle Charlie's apartment and had a great time touring Chicago on my weekend off.

Terry and I didn't have much time alone under the circumstances, but just having her there was great. I didn't want the four days to end. I wanted to quit work and go home but I couldn't. I needed the money for college. Although the work environment at the box company was becoming unbearable, I was determined to ignore the other employees' rude treatment of me and stick with the job for the rest of the summer. One man in particular, Craw Biddle, hated me, but I actually had one friend, an older gentleman from Poland whom I called Gorz, abbreviation for his last name Gorzynski. We took all our breaks together.

The day after Terry left, the insults at work became absurd.

"Hey, yellow belly, why don't you meet Craw out on the dock at lunch break?" one of the boys, a greasy looking little wimp, whispered to me as he walked by. This was the most absurd thing I had ever experienced. I had never said or done anything to these guys and they were making a routine out of harassing me.

One night Craw drove by me on the forklift to say, "the boys tell me you wanna take me on. That right Yankee boy?"

"No, it's not right," I said. "I'm not interested in fighting you or anyone else." I gritted my teeth. This was very difficult for me to do. I grew up unable to back down from a fight. Defending myself was ingrained in me.

"Your Daddy a chicken shit like you, Yankee boy?"

That was it. My patience had run out. I had to either fight or quit work. Craw had pushed the ultimate button.

"South parking lot, right after work," I said with a direct look back at Craw. Better to get my butt kicked, I decided, than to live through more of this harassment.

After weeks of my ignoring the challenges and insults, my sudden and abrupt response came as a surprise to Crawford Biddle. Gorz urged me not to do it. "He a mean guy. Not smart you to fight him."

In my mind, I didn't feel that I had a choice. As I made my way to the south parking lot, I noticed that a crowd of about a dozen workers were gathered together. They were smiling, ready to watch the slaughter.

Gorz stood off to the side behind a car, shaking his head as if to again say, don't do it. But I had to now. I could see no turning back. I remembered the feeling of that Golden Gloves boxing match when it felt like an invisible bowling ball was slamming into my stomach and baseball bat was connecting with my jaw. I feared the same from Craw.

Craw walked toward me, a mean look on his face. I raised my hands, left hand and left foot forward. I circled to his left. I was surprised that he was flat-footed, not moving at all on his feet. Craw was no Golden-Glover.

"Take em out, Craw, take his head off, kill that Yankee boy," Craw's supporters chanted.

Craw lashed out with a vicious right at my face. I ducked, but the blow caught the top edge of my head at the hairline. It stung. I took notice that my opponent stumbled when he threw his punch. He was a bull, I concluded, but certainly not one with any polished boxing skills.

"You fighting or dancing?" Craw barked out.

"Quit running, Yankee boy," a spectator yelled.

I saw the next punch coming, sidestepped and found an opening. I slipped in my right to his face and caught him flush on the nose. Craws big frame didn't budge, but blood trickled from his nose. He wiped the blood with his hand, looked at it and came at me raging, catching me with a punch on my ear. I heard bells ringing. I circled him faster, trying to avoid another of his wicked blows. This guy could punch with power. My only chance was to keep my distance, make him miss, and then counter punch.

"Security, security," several spectators yelled out. Plant security came driving up to the scene.

"Break it up, now. Go home." Two uniformed men jumped from their car.

The group scattered. Gorz yelled for me to come to him. He drove me home. My ear was bleeding and I had a lump on my forehead. My heart was pounding, my hands shaking. Three aspirins didn't help. It took two hours for me to get to sleep.

I returned to work the next day with apprehension. I was amazed that Craw and the boys never bothered me again. I suspect they were warned by security and management. Or, maybe I gained some respect. My friend Gorz told me that he thought I was winning the fight. I don't think so. I was lucky security came.

My last day of work at the end of August was a happy day for me. Gorz was the only worker who knew I was quitting. As I walked through the parking lot I spotted the little antagonizer who was so insistent on arranging for me to fight his hero, Craw. I couldn't resist.

"Hey Steve," I addressed the greasy little wimp guy by name for the first time. "Tell Craw, I am going to kick his ass when I come to work tomorrow." With a look of disbelief, little Stevie turned to me and said, "I will to tell Craw all right. He will kill you this time."

I laughed. I already had my final check. I would never see that bunch again. I couldn't wait to get home to see Terry. I was inspired, more than ever, to advance my education. Factory life wasn't for me.

Brother Trouble

While I was away for the summer, working in Chicago, my brother Lavern was released from Jackson Prison for good behavior. Lavern had taken up reading the Bible and had even been assigned to preaching to other prisoners. He was released with a commitment that he wanted to spread the word of Jesus. He moved into my parents' home.

I doubt that he saved any souls, but he did save a pregnant lady by the name of Nancy Hardenburg. Nancy was four months pregnant when Lavern met her. A nice looking lady, brunette hair and a pretty smile, in desperate need of a husband. They were married after two weeks of dating. Lavern and Nancy came to Chicago and moved in with me and Uncle Charlie. Lavern found a job in a warehouse on his first day in his new city. Two weeks later though he was fired for drinking on the job. Out of a job, Uncle Charlie asked Lavern to leave. He returned to Muskegon. The new wife, Nancy, ran out of patience. She had a last name for her baby, but not a provider. Nancy went her separate way.

On his second week back in Muskegon, Lavern was arrested for drunk and disorderly. Appearing before the judge, he gave a religious plea that earned another chance to come back to my parent's home on a plea by my father that he would be responsible to keep him away from alcohol and off the streets.

One week after Lavern's latest release, he talked my Dad into taking him downtown to watch a parade. Dad wasn't a very competent chaperone. Lavern could sneak alcohol behind my dad's back or slip away without him realizing what was going on. While at the parade, my dad looked around in the crowd, unable to find his oldest son. Not being able to find your son in a crowd is something that should be of concern for a small child, not a twenty-seven year old; but Lavern was a child in a man's body.

"Ho, ho hum, I'm just a bum. Ho, ho hum, I'm just a bum." My dad had spotted him now. Lavern was in the parade; marching in front of the band, staggering but arms swinging, knees rising like he was the leader of the band. As usual, his stardom only lasted a couple of minutes.

Dad watched helplessly as the police hauled Lavern away to the Muskegon County Jail. A few days later he was on his way back to Jackson Prison where he again found the Lord. He said that he didn't remember what happened. He concluded that the Lord must have wanted him to return to Jackson to preach to the prisoners. Within a year, Lavern was out of Jackson again, on the promise to deliver the Lord's message. And again, my Mother said, "Lavern is going to be ok now. He's going to be a preacher."

A few days after being released from Jackson, Lavern called his magazine sales friend, Jerry Gutnik. Gutnik bought him a bus ticket to Chicago. We didn't hear from Lavern again for two years.

My second year at Ferris was briefly interrupted when my Dad called to tell me that my brother Gerald was in trouble. A girl that Gerald had dated two times became pregnant and claimed the pregnancy came as a result of an non-consensual sexual encounter. He denied, but faced charges based on the girl's claims. Knowing that he could face serious jail time, I came home to help with the investigation and to help him with his attorney. Because of his inability to read, Gerald had difficulty with the forms and with communicating with his attorney.

My first decision was to try to solve his reading problem, a problem that I concluded he had been living with unnecessarily. I did some research on adults with reading handicaps and discovered than many adults couldn't read simply because they had not been taught properly. Recalling the poor teaching skills of Garnet Lindgren, I decided that Gerald should go to an adult reading tutor. After hours of persuasion I was able to convince Gerald to take the reading lessons. Three months later Gerald had a new life. He could read. He never became proficient, but was able to read signs and to slowly read newspapers.

I drove back and forth from Ferris several times a week to help with the trial. My grades suffered, but I managed to avoid dropping out of school. The trial took place before a fair-minded judge who decided the relationship was consensual. His decision was to order Gerald to pay expenses for the girl to give birth to the baby, and place the baby out for adoption.

Gerald didn't have any interest in knowing about the baby's adoption. In his mind he was concerned that he had fathered a child that might inherit his learning handicap. My dad loaned Gerald the money for the costs that he was ordered to pay. Always motivated to be self-sufficient, Gerald ultimately paid back every penny that he borrowed from my dad.

And, he didn't give up. As a result of his new reading skills, Gerald was able to obtain a good paying factory job in Muskegon at Johnson's Products as an assembly line worker.

"Yes."

On Christmas eve of 1961, I got the biggest gift of my young life, Terry accepted my proposal and we planned a June wedding. I finished my second year at Ferris as Sports Editor of the Ferris Torch. I continued my habit of attaining A grades in the subject I liked and C grades in subjects I found boring. My grade point and entrance test scores allowed me to get accepted at Michigan State University.

Ma and Dad were proud and excited that I was attending college. They were ecstatic when I told them that Terry and I planned to get married. We wanted and had a nice wedding. That most special day in my life was a thrill. Gerald was my best man and Terry's twin, Cherri, was her bridesmaid. A big reception was my mother's idea. She never had much of a wedding for herself and neither of my older brothers were married, so this was her chance to enjoy a family wedding. Dad would rather have given Terry and me some money. My mother got her way. A dance hall was rented and we partied with about 300 guests.

Terry and I skipped out at 11 that night and headed north for a Mackinaw Island honeymoon, 120 miles north. We only drove for about 30 minutes before stopping at a motel. Now this may sound unbelievable, but after five years of dating, this was our first time sleeping together. Terry's Mom was a little old-fashioned about pre-marital relationships, drilling into her daughter's head that the wedding night was special and should be the first time to sleep together. I can only say, Trudy was right, it was special.

Terry got a job as a telephone operator. I got a summer job maintaining the grounds at the Muskegon Standard Oil distribution center. Our jobs went well, but our first apartment was a joke. Looking to keep our expenses down, we rented a little one bedroom apartment that was an addition off the back of an elderly widow's home. Within a week we suspected our landlord was using her key to come into our apartment while we were at work.

I verified my suspicion when I found that a tiny piece of thread that I had run across the top of the door had been broken when

I came home. I immediately called a locksmith to have the lock changed. Our landlord's reaction was to call the police the next day. She was informed by the police that, we, as renters, had a right to change the lock. Our landlord didn't bother us anymore after that. In the fall of 1962, Terry and I moved into Spartan Village, Michigan State University's married student housing. What a deal—$85 per month including utilities.

Terry got a part time job at Sears and I got a job in East Lansing restaurant, Warren's Prime. Terry had a tuition scholarship so costs were low. I entered the school of journalism and Terry enrolled in the school of education.

Our 450 square-foot apartment was composed of a living room, kitchen, bathroom, and a bedroom, all enclosed by walls thin enough to hear the voices of apartments A and C on either side of us. I especially remember the couple in apartment A, Tom and Karen. They fought frequently, too frequently for our comfort. One night Tom came home half loaded.

"You're a f- - - - - - drunk. Get your lazy ass out of here."

Two minutes after Tom had stormed out the door, Karen, all alone now, began crying out, "Tom, please come home, please come home." She continued this same plea on and on, making it impossible for Terry and me to sleep. Finally, two hours later Tom came home, now fully loaded. But, we were actually relieved. Karen got her wish. Tom had returned. Hopefully they would make up and shut up, so we could get some sleep.

'Where you been? You f - - - - - - drunk. Why did you come back?"

So, I'm sure you can guess what Tom does. He is out the door again, tires squealing as he drives off.

"Oh no, not again," I said to Terry, as Karen started yelling out, "Tom, come home, please come home" again.

The next time Tom came back I was ready to pound on the wall and say, "He's back, now shut to f - - - up," but we just put up with it, managing only a few hours sleep that night. It certainly made us appreciate each other, and our relationship, how kind we always were to each other.

While working on the Michigan State News, a daily newspaper, I covered sports. On assignments to cover football games I became acquainted with sports writers for newspapers from around the state. I was amazed to learn how little money they made. I was more disenchanted to hear that I could expect to work twenty years before having a chance to become a Sports Editor.

About the time I was becoming discouraged with the earning opportunities as a sports writer, I was being encouraged by Mr.Warren at Warren's Prime. I was hired as a bus boy. Bus boys make tips at the discretion of the waitress' willingness to share some of their tips. I came to work early, looking for ways to impress the waitresses. I set tables, made sure salt and pepper shakers were full, swept floors, made coffee, and of course cleared and reset tables.

I can't say I enjoyed what I was doing, but the faster I worked the faster the time went by, and the more the waitresses shared their tips. One night the dishwasher didn't show up. I jumped in. The dishwasher was fired and I was asked to come back the next night to cover again, and again the next night. This wasn't good. Dishwashers don't make tips.

What I did get was Mr. Warren's appreciation. After four days of washing dishes I was given an hourly rate raise and moved in to work with the cooks. Now, this was still not working too well financially, since beginning cooks don't make tips either. After one day on the cook's line, Mr. Warren called me into his office. He urged me to consider a career in restaurant management.

"You could become a manager in less than five years. When I learned that most hotel and restaurant managers make more money than most sports editors I was sold on the idea. Why, I reasoned, should I wait twenty years for a job that paid less than one I could attain in only five? The next week I changed my major to Hotel and Restaurant Management. I continued to work for Mr. Warren. I worked every position in the kitchen, including lead cook and running the wheel.

The wheelman coordinates orders between the kitchen and service staff and is the toughest job in the kitchen. I was the first person Mr. Warren called when one of the other cooks didn't show. He knew he could count on me.

Beginning my second year at Warren's Prime, I realized I needed to diversify my experience. Kellogg Center, an on-campus

University owned hotel and restaurant, became the logical choice. I told Mr. Edwards, when he interviewed me, that I would take any job as I wanted to experience everything.

They started me as bellboy, a job that anyone with ambition can get a handle on within a few days. When I said I wanted to learn every job, Warren took my word for it. I worked the coat-check room, helped the night shift janitor, helped clean rooms, and helped the maintenance man on several projects. Remembering from my interview that I had washed dishes, Mr. Edwards had me on the dishwasher a couple nights, too.

At my request, after a couple months, I was moved to the front desk. On several occasions, while working the night shift, I stayed all night on my own time to learn the night audit procedure. Mr. Edwards told me that I had experienced more jobs than any employee who ever worked for him. I tried to do the same for every company I worked for, and felt that it was time well spent.

Terry carried a heavy load of classes, enabling her to obtain a teaching job after just three years of college. She was only one class short of earning her degree and took that class while teaching in Mason, a little town five miles from the MSU campus. I graduated one semester late, but with a lot of hours of valuable work experience. When I graduated in December of 1964, I had a resume I was proud of, with excellent recommendations from my professors and employers. With Terry's teaching job, and my part time work, we finally had money to spend and treated ourselves to a new car. We were ready to move on. Job offers were plentiful; management training programs at restaurant chains, hotels, hospitals, and clubs.

All but one of my seven interviews, a country club management position, involved working in some type of program that would take two to three years to achieve management. Impatiently and contrary to the advice of my school advisors I wanted to interview for the club job. They suggested that I would be wasting my time to expect an offer and that even if I did get an offer to go directly into management I would be "jumping the gun."

By that time I already had six job offers and so "jumping the gun' didn't register with me as much of a problem. I was given the proper advice, but decided to consider all options.

In measuring our years at Michigan State, we could not have made a better choice; a great value, a beautiful campus, a broad education that prepared me for a career and employment opportunities not only as a new graduate, but also as an alumnus, as my career changed in later years.

Terry and Wayne, wedding, June 16th, 1962.

Wayne in dorm room at Ferris, 1961

Terry and Wayne, Muskegon HS graduation photos.

Terry Got It Right

A small entrance sign read "Warwick Hills Golf & Country Club." I parked my Mustang in the back of the lot, realizing that my car, a Ford, might not be very popular at the "Home of the Buick Open." My little buggy was the only non-General Motors car in the lot.

Warwick is a beautiful property on a hill just south of Grand Blanc, Michigan; the home of a former large wealthy residential estate, remodeled to accommodate member dining, and overlooking a nationally known golf course. The club's fame came from hosting the Buick Open, one of the largest professional tournaments on the PGA tour. At that time, the $100,000 purse was the third largest on the whole tour.

I felt intimidated walking into the small meeting room; it was oval shaped, and about the size of a bedroom, probably a home library before the building was converted into the clubhouse. The management committee's board members were occupying four high back leather executive chairs comfortably spaced around a round mahogany table. They were Club President, Phil Hall of Hall Steel, House Chairman, Dr. Joe Batdorf, Bruce Pollack of Pollack Real Estate, and Joe Ross, a CPA and one of the early developers of H&R Block.

These men all stood up to introduce themselves to me and shake my hand. All taller than I, they seemed to be in their early forties and appeared to me to be quite an impressive group. Very business like, dressed in suits or sport coats and a tie; they smiled and asked me to have a seat.

As a first impression, I felt outclassed and apprehensive at how they would proceed with the interview. Would they expect me to know a lot about country clubs and golf? I never played the game in my life. Frankly, at the time, I didn't understand why anyone would want to spend so much money chasing around a little white ball; a rich guys game.

I concealed my apprehension, intending to show self-confidence. They all had my resume and had to know that my experience didn't include working in a country club. This interview is just for the experience, I said to myself. I had never been to a country club before. I had already narrowed my job offers down to three management trainee positions; an airline food company in Chicago, a Southern California Restaurant chain, or Hilton Hotels.

Never having been very far away from Michigan, the West Coast sounded exciting. The airline job involved some free travel, and Hilton was the big name opportunity.

When I had told my advisor that I was going for the Warwick interview, he told me, "Clubs are tough. You don't have the experience to be seriously considered at Warwick. Besides, they go through managers like most places go through dish washers."

Separately, I had confirmed that. Warwick was founded in the mid-1950s and had employed eleven different managers in ten years. Their current manager was both golf pro and club manager. Apparently, he was not very skilled in food operations; the board's latest plan was to hire a clubhouse manager to take care of food operations so that he could focus on the golf part of his job.

"Well, Mr. Lobdell, we have talked to a lot of candidates for this position and you are the youngest and least experienced. Do you feel you are qualified for this job?" quizzed President Hall. *Why am I here? I thought to myself.*

"If I understand the job description correctly, you want a restaurant and club activities manager," I said calmly. "I believe I would enjoy the challenge and could do a good job for you. I can assure you that I am not a golfer and have absolutely no knowledge of golf operations."

Dr. Batdorf was next. I had good vibes about him. He was the friendliest, and looked me in the eyes with an expression of interest.

"I notice you have excellent recommendations and I spoke with Mr. Warren at Warren's Prime Restaurant. He said you were his best kitchen employee, and that you had good management potential. Yet, you really haven't had actual management experience. Do you feel your classes at Michigan State prepared you to manage?" he asked.

"MSU has the best Hospitality Management program in the country and I was one of the leaders in my management classes," I told him. "Although you are correct that I have not had full charge management experience, I think I am ready to manage."

From that point I added some textbook principles of management. Then I zinged in a comment that I would get a lot of help from my friend, Ted Donns, at Flint Golf Club. The Flint Club, eight miles across town, was a larger club than Warwick and Donns was highly regarded there as the manager for over five years.

"Ted is a friend of yours? How long have you known Ted?" quizzed Joe Ross. Ross and Hall belonged to the Flint club as well as Warwick.

"About two hours." I smiled. "I arranged an appointment to meet him just before coming here. He was very helpful and indicated that, if I got this job, he would be pleased to have me call him anytime" I could see that I was getting their attention. My confidence was rising. I was starting to have fun.

My interviewers looked at me, and at each other, with expressions that seemed to indicate they were impressed with my initiative.

They proceeded to ask typical interview questions—grades, past experience, marriage status, plans for a family, and details about each of my jobs. I was then given an opportunity to ask them questions about the club and the responsibilities of the job.

"Who does your Manager report to?" Donns had advised me that past Warwick managers had to cope with too many bosses.

"The Board of Directors, primarily Dr. Batdorf. He is our House Chairman," Hall offered.

"I understand that I would be working in the interest of the entire club and, in particular the Board of Directors. However, if I were fortunate enough to be offered this position and chose to accept, I would request an understanding that I only take direction from one person. I believe that would be in your best interest to help me avoid any confusion as to my responsibilities." At this point, I was wondering if I was pushing it.

At the conclusion of the interview I was given a tour, which included an inspection of the kitchen and the accounting office. In response to an offer for any other questions, I requested a menu and asked to review the financials and some supplier invoices. Before leaving, I asked if I could discuss the financials and my observations about the kitchen and supplier invoices. I could hardly believe what I had found as result of my tour of the kitchen and review of the invoices.

Mr. Ross was the only member of the interview team remaining and he led me back to the small meeting room. At the risk of offending the club, I suggested that, while I recognized that most country clubs expect to lose money in their food and bar operations, Warwick was out of line with what was standard for both food and labor costs.

I didn't mention that I didn't see a time clock, an elementary necessity for labor accounting. But, I couldn't resist telling Mr., Ross, a numbers man, what I saw on one of the invoices. The grocery supplier's previous day delivery had charged the club for fifty packages of cheese in five-pound packages. I had specifically recalled seeing five packages and thought that even five packages seemed a bit much for their menu. No way would they have fifty. I also knew that supplier overcharging tricks included invoicing in a way that, if noticed, could simply be credited as a typing error of fifty instead of five.

"I assume a typing error," I politely suggested to Mr. Ross.

"I suppose," Mr. Ross added with a frown.

Concluding the meeting with Mr. Ross, I was on my way back to East Lansing. I had just had a fun and educational Saturday. I was now ready to accept one of my other three choices. I favored the move to California.

That evening, Terry and I started talking about plans to move to the West Coast. Could she find a teaching job in the Los Angeles area? How would my beginning salary of $6,000 a year cover us? Would we be able to find an apartment that we could afford? Our plans were placed on hold with a Monday evening phone call.

"Our management committee was very impressed with your interview and the recommendations from your references. We are very interested in considering you for the position as Manager at Warwick and would like you to return next Saturday for a second interview."

"I am pleased to hear from you Dr. Batdorf," I said right away. "I would be happy to come back this Saturday."

I was further surprised with Dr. Batdorf's request that I bring my wife to join in the interview.

Terry and I returned to Warwick Hills that Saturday without the slightest idea of what the second interview would involve and what they would expect of my new wife. We found out the key question early in the interview.

"Terry, how would you be expected to be involved in your husband's job if he were to take the position of manager here at Warwick?" asked Dr. Batdorf.

Terry paused, and then hit a home run, as far as I was concerned.

"Well, Dr. Batdorf, I plan to teach school," she said. "I understand club managers work long hours, weekends and evenings. I am prepared for that and I would support Wayne by understanding the responsibilities he would have. As for involvement, I would not have any. I will have plenty to do with my own job."

I later learned that several of Warwick's past managers had problems with their wives involvement in the club, an experience the board wanted to avoid with any future manager.

Dr. Batdorf's next question," Do you plan to have a family?" got a quick chuckle and comment from President Hall.

"Dr. Batdorf is a pediatrician. He's looking for business."

Terry indicated that we did plan to have children at some point. A few more basic questions, a tour of a residential home that the club owned, and then came the offer. $7,200 per year plus benefits, including use of the home.

"Oh, and one more thing," added Mr. Hall with a smile, "we would like you to sell that Mustang that you have been parking at the back of the lot. We will arrange for a Buick dealer to sell you your choice of a Buick at factory cost." I accepted the job.

I had to hold back tears as Terry and I drove away from Warwick that day. Terry could find a teaching job for $4,500 to $5,000, which would put us over $10,000 in income—and with very little expenses. I was thrilled. The hours would be long; the job stressful, but we were on our way. The hard work was now going to pay off.

A Vision

I woke early Sunday morning in our 1443B Spartan Village apartment, looking out the window with one of those moments of reflection on the path my life had taken me on. It was a pleasant day as December days go in Michigan. Just cold enough for white snowflakes to appear from the sky, melting as they hit the warmth of the sidewalk between the window and our little blue Mustang parked out front.

We had first spotted that little Mustang in November, parked in a corral on display out front of the East Lansing Ford dealership. Terry had a job teaching school and I had my part time restaurant jobs. A new car wasn't in our budget, but we had to have it. Well, at least I did.

I was full of energy that snowy morning, looking out the window. Full of excitement about the job I had just landed, I knew my life had just shifted gears just like slipping that straight stick Mustang from first to second. I'm not sure how long I stood there. Years flew through my mind like the Mustang zipping through Spartan Village on my way to class.

I knew now how my dad felt when he finally got the farm that he had worked so hard for. Thinking about what Terry and my combined salaries would be, my mother and dad didn't have anything close to what we would have. Yet, they were just as successful and happy. Just like us, they were on their way to realizing their dream.

I recalled those years on the farm; mean spirited Mrs. Lindgren, Mrs. Bennett who didn't have a clue about me when she made me repeat 5th grade, and uppity Mr. Wagoner. I also remembered clearly my narrow escapes in the hood. I wanted right then to go back to some of those people and say, "I have proven you wrong."

Mr. May knew. Ma and Dad knew, even though they didn't know how to point the way. Terry knew. Most of all, I knew that I was going to succeed in whatever path I chose, and provide a good life for Terry and the family we would some day have. Our kids would not have to face a Mrs. Lindgren or a Mrs. Bennet. They would have Terry and me encouraging them and providing them with a loving environment. And, they would not be born in a basement.

I knew my goals would not be easy. I was prepared for bumps along the way. Just like my Dad, I would work harder. Only, I would do it with an education and the confidence I had in my ability to motivate and lead others in a teamwork approach to management.

Launching My Career

Of all the faces at Warwick Hills, the only ones younger than mine were the bus boys. This thought occurred to me one night as I passed by the bathroom, glanced at my reflection in the mirror, and collapsed into bed. It was late, I was not a bus boy but the manager of the whole place, and despite being completely exhausted, my mind was racing. It was the end of my first day on the job, and I had spent it observing, evaluating, and trying to learn everyone's name. Despite the bravado I showed in the interview, I was worried that I was in a little over my head.

The employees acted apprehensive around me, but I had the good sense to make an ally out of one of them right away. My first target was the hostess, Hazel, a veteran at the club, she seated the members, mixed drinks when needed, waited on tables at times, and knew all the members by name as well as their likes and dislikes. Hazel could tell you where they liked to sit, what they usually ordered, and even which of the men expected a little extra pour in their cocktail.

One of the small dining room windows looked out onto the club's parking lot. Whenever I had a chance, I'd ask Hazel to take a peak and let me know who was coming.

"Good evening Mrs. Dinger, Mr. Dinger," I'd say, as they walked through the front door, thanks to Hazel's prompting. This little game always got their attention, especially if I hadn't met them before.

Herm, the Chef, "Mama" the baker, and the other cooks were old enough to be my parents. The little pad and pencil that I carried around made them nervous, as if I might be writing down their shortcomings. It shouldn't have though; in those first few days I was only scribbling notes to help me remember the members' names. I wrote, "Mrs. X looks like Lucy Ricardo, Mr. Y is bald and pudgy, Mr. Z is a tall, loud guy with glasses, and Mr. C is the happy Greek."

As the days wore on, I also made a few notes about the portioning inconsistencies I spotted; not only Hazel's extra pours, but Chef Herm's variations in portioning and Mama preparing larger quantities than needed. The quality was excellent and the service was great; they just had not been taught portion consistency and a system for projecting quantity needs. The staff had excellent skills and good attitudes; they were just never trained to emphasize operational efficiencies. That was what I was supposed to take care of. Still, I knew they wouldn't be eager to have some young "whipper-snapper," a college boy, start giving them new rules. I'd have to be diplomatic.

I told Hazel that I was a little rusty on pouring drinks and asked that she demonstrate how she managed to pour so accurately. Over the course of a couple weeks, with a few more hints and compliments, Hazel's consistencies improved. She had a lot of energy in her slightly rotund 5'2" frame. Her thick, dark-rimmed glasses were no obstacle in her talent for total dining room awareness. Hazel had an almost military accuracy for status and location. With her back to the room she could whisper to me each member's name and where they were sitting. Eventually, with her help, I was able to move through the dining room and address any table by name; a must for a good club manager.

The office had an accumulation of records on past daily lunch and dinner counts, including club activities. This data had been painstakingly filed, but never used. Using such information for projecting staffing and food quantity preparation is a fairly common practice in restaurants. As incentive, I started putting $2 in a jar every Monday to be given to the best forecaster of the week. It was usually won by Hazel.

With Chef Herm however, a challenge worked best to inspire him to attend to detail. "Hey Chef, see how close you can come to 8 oz. on your next slice," I'd say, when he was carving meat. Then I'd check him out on the new portions scale I just bought. He was right on. I tried one, went over 9 oz., and got a grin in return from Chef Herm. After that, I challenged him from time to time on other portioning. He usually won. And, our portion consistency improved.

The new routine that irritated Hazel and Chef Herm most though was the weekly inventory; they already dreaded their monthly inventories before I even arrived and now I was making them do it every week. On occasion, I did an inventory and cost calculation mid-week. That was, I overheard someone whisper, "a crazy waste of time." Weekly meetings to review my spreadsheet calculations and point out improvements, and my promise to return to monthly inventories as soon as we achieved our cost targets, soon eased their reluctance.

My goals for the club were just beginning to take shape when I faced the biggest challenge of my young career: Managing club food operations for the Buick Open. Excitement for the tournament began weeks in advance with PGA officials and network television people preparing for the nationally-televised event. The 1965 tournament included most of the top players on the tour. Gary Player, Sam Snead, Arnold Palmer, and Jack Nicklaus were all participants. More than 100,000 spectators paid $1 at the gate. Crowds of spectators even came to watch the players practice on Monday and Tuesday.

In those days, Warwick didn't have a driving range, just a big open field that golfers could use – if they didn't mind retrieving their own balls. Watching the pros was an amusing sight. A line of pros fired off shots to their respective burlap bag carrying caddies, scattered out in the field one, two, or two hundred fifty yards away. One bold young caddie, Benny, was assigned to Sam Snead, who was at the 100-yard range to work on his wedge shot. Benny stood out there bravely, held his side pant's pocket open, and yelled, "Come on Sammy, right here." The crowd cheered when Sam's shot bounced off Benny's hip.

For me, the Buick Open's big event was not the golf tournament, it was the Pro-Am dinner. Buick flew a private jet to Hollywood to pick up celebrities to join the pros and members in a Wednesday pre-tournament practice game called the "Buick Open Pro-Am." The cocktail and dinner party that followed was too large for the Warwick Clubhouse to handle. My solution was to order a large tent, have it set up outside, and serve an extravagant buffet. I pestered Hazel and Chef Herm daily for two weeks in advance with details for elaborate hors d'ouevres and ice carvings to go with the buffet of fancy salads, shrimp, roast pig, and prime rib. Mama the baker promised, and delivered, the best-looking dessert table that I had ever seen. Famous singers Perry Como, Andy Williams, Gordon MacRae, and comedian "Lonesome George Goebel" were among the celebrities who stayed until midnight to enjoy the fun.

Driving home at 2 a.m. after a successful night like this, my mind often wandered back to those years on the farm and my narrow escape from the rough streets of Muskegon. I recognized how lucky I was to be going home to Terry, the person who helped me find my way.

I was lucky in other ways though, too. In restaurant management, a lousy predecessor makes you an easy hero. Some basic emphasis on consistency, improved projections, tighter staff scheduling, and comparison shopping between suppliers resulted in some very noticeable improvements in the food and bar operation financials. Eight months into my job, I was given a handsome raise. A week later though, I made my first significant management mistake.

"Where's my table?" A serious looking Mrs. Dinger came prancing into the kitchen at noon on a September Saturday. I gave her a stunned look, while I rattled my brain.

" I have eighteen for 12:15," she said. "Sixteen prime rib and two shrimp."

"And, you booked this with?' I asked her, feeling confused.

"You," Mrs. Dinger said. "I booked it with you. Two weeks ago. I talked to you at the ladies golf luncheon. And I confirmed it with a call to the office on Thursday."

I had no recollection of this conversation. None. But no discussion was needed. I apologized and assured her we would take care of her. Hazel was already hustling to set up the table. We didn't have any prime rib and Chef Herm wasn't scheduled until later, so I personally broiled New York Strips to order. Mrs. Dinger calmed down and was very understanding, but she liked to talk and word of this oversight sure got around.

I don't recall how the booking got missed, but I know it never happened again. Mrs. Dinger, as well as most of the other members, were great to work for. I joined the national Club Manager's Association, where I was the youngest member from Michigan. In my third year, I began to receive an occasional call from recruiters seeking a manager for another club. Only one interested me enough to go for an interview; Traverse City Golf and Country Club.

I fell in love with the town. With the quaint little city, the crystal clear inland lakes, and the big beautiful bays off Lake Michigan. The problem was that I was too ambitious to come to Traverse City. The place had physical beauty but was known for it's low salaries in many types of jobs; "half the pay for a view of the bay" was how people described it. I returned to Warwick wishing I could someday bring my family to a place like Traverse City.

Still, I enjoyed my job at Warwick. Club management provided a long career and a good life for many other managers I met in the association. Frankly though, the guys that intrigued me most were some of the members. Dr. Joe Batdorf, House Committee Chairman, was my favorite. He treated me like a son. Of course, I had no interest in becoming a doctor. But, the businessmen, the manufacturers, real estate developers, and stockbrokers, were who really fascinated me. Their life and success was all about leadership, seeking new ideas, hard work, and finding and motivating good people.

Another of my favorites, Mr. Chinonis, made a lot of money moving in and out of Chrysler stock. Mr. Hall started manufacturing parts for steel companies then bought a steel factory. Mr. Pollack made his mark in real estate. I also remember a couple guys who were not so nice. I will refer to them as Mr. Lamb and Mr. Bark. Lamb was a boaster. I don't recall his profession but I suspected he was all talk and no show. As a club member, he was a frequent complainer about the service he received and the portions he was served. Mr. Bark was very wealthy and everybody knew it. They knew it because he told everybody, at every opportunity.

Mr. Lamb was one of three notable antagonists I dealt with during my time at Warwick. I suspected that each of them overextended themselves to belong to the club. They complained about portion sizes when I established a system for portion consistency. They complained when I closed the 19th hole bar at 10 p.m., enough though they were the only patrons who ever stayed after 9. They didn't like the new menu. One day their meal wasn't warm enough, and the next it was overcooked.

For the most part, I tried to accommodate their demands or referred them to Dr. Batdorf. I did have one close encounter. One afternoon, Lamb demanded that the 19th hole bar, called the Pine Room, had overcharged him. I checked the record with the bartender, and verified with him that Mr. Lamb had not been overcharged. I told him that the records were correct, but that the club would buy him another drink the next time when he came in from golf.

"I don't want your charity and you don't call me a liar," Lamb demanded.

"Sir," I said, keeping my voice calm, " I'm just telling you what the records show."

"Listen boy!" Lamb shouted, "I'm the member, you're my employee."

"Look Sir, I am just telling you what I know, and what I can do," I answered. "If you don't like what I do, go to the Board. File a complaint."

"How would you like to get knocked on your ass?" he retorted.

Physically, Mr. Lamb didn't seem like much of a threat to me. He was a couple inches taller than me, about thirty-five years old, with a little extra around the belt. I found time to work out and even though I didn't box anymore, I was still in as good of shape as ever. In retrospect, I should have walked away. Unfortunately, I didn't grow up learning the sensible thing to do in the face of a bully. My instincts wouldn't allow me to turn my heels in retreat.

Instead, I took off my sport coat and tossed it onto the carpet. The only witness to this incident was an assistant golf pro. I moved my left foot forward, planted my feet firmly, and raised my hands in a defensive position. I was prepared to take the first shot. I didn't have to. Mr. Lamb stopped well short of me and said, "Anytime you want to mess with me, just let me know."

At that, he turned and walked away. I was relieved. A fist fight with a member wouldn't look good on my resume.

As for Mr. Bark, "Mr. big bucks," who owned several factories, I can best describe him as nothing more than an arrogant and inconsiderate jerk. He joined the club soon after I became manager and, with all his influence, immediately became a board member.

"Hey come here," he called to me one evening, with a condescending flip of his finger. He was having dinner with some business associates. I politely came to his table, moving from where I had been standing to observe the dining room.

"See that table over there?" he questioned. I looked at a table that had been vacated just a few minutes earlier. I knew a waitress was on her way to clean it.

"It needs cleaning and you look like you need something to do." He gave a sharp pointing gesture at the table. "And tell Hazel I want another salad. This lettuce is not crisp enough."

I wanted to tell Mr. Bark to go to hell. Instead, I just took a deep breath and pointed to the waitress who was on her way to take care of the table, then asked Hazel to bring him a fresh salad. I had, as manager, cleaned tables many times when needed, but not on an impolite demand. Mr. Bark wanted to show his associates how important he was. I doubted that they, or anyone else in the dining room, wanted to see such rude behavior.

Bark and Lamb represented a rare exception to an otherwise great educational experience with a terrific membership at Warwick Hills. I am forever appreciative of the opportunity they gave me to launch my career.

As I recall those incidents did have a purpose, though. I began thinking about considering other career options. I couldn't become a doctor like Dr. Batdorf and I didn't have the money for land development. I sure couldn't buy a manufacturing business, either.

But somehow, some way I wanted to find the path to a business ownership. Having grown up on a small farm and survived the hood I saw ownership as the way to secure a better future for Terry and the family we wanted. I couldn't visualize the path to that goal, but I became committed to finding my way.

Epilogue

Shifting Gears

Looking back, my Climb from The Cellar to my first management job was a memorable journey. Here are some highlights of what happened to me and Terry and to our family, and to my parents and my brothers. Some of it's triumphant, some tragic, some bittersweet.

After three years of an enjoyable and educating experience at Warwick Hills I decided the time had come to move on. Once I had the desire to forge a career in business, I just could no longer be satisfied having other people call my shots. Believe it or not, Mr. Bark later became Club President and pulled the same trick on my successor, Pete Siagras, as he had on me. Pete wasn't as patient as I was though; he handed Mr. Bark his keys and walked off the job.

I did leave Warwick, but not to become a doctor or a manufacturing tycoon, both of which were impractical and out of my reach. There was one career that I learned about through getting to know some of the Warwick members that I could see myself doing. I could become a stockbroker. So, that's what I did.

I left the security of my club management career behind and started on a path that led to fifteen years of career changes, ups and downs, borderline bankruptcy, eighty-plus hour weeks in a gradual journey to reach my American dream.

I joined the Flint, Michigan office of the Francis I. DuPont's stock and bond firm on a $600.00 per month training salary. After the training the $600.00 became a draw against commissions. The tough part was leaving Terry and our two sons behind for fourteen weeks of training in New York City. I made the best of my time though, finishing second among a class of thirty-two trainees from across the country. Jubilant, I returned to the Flint office only to learn that the branch manager turned out to be more of a commission pusher than an investment advisor.

"I already have a broker. I don't have any money to invest. Can you guarantee me a winner? Do you have any inside information? Is the market going up or down tomorrow? Not interested." I heard these words, and many others, on the phone everyday when I'd call prospective clients. Sometimes, people would just hang up. Cold calling wore on me until I didn't want to make one more call. Ever. Then on my fourth night, I got Mr. Rollins.

"You're just the man the wife and I been looking for," a friendly voice said on the other end of the line. "Can you come over now?"

It sounded almost too easy to me, but I needed a change of pace from the grind of sitting at my desk listening to rejections.

"Sure, Mr. Rollins," I said right away. "I just have to return a call to one of my clients and I'll be on my way." A little fib.

I checked the address. By the part of town Mr. Rollins lived in, I suspected I was going to be wasting my time. Still, I needed practice on my presentation, so off I went.

When I arrived at the Rollins' little old house, I considered turning back. I could have just told them about the $500 minimum investment, because I was sure that would have given me a quick exit.

The Rollins were sitting on the porch. The porch light was not on, one of the porch steps was missing, and some of the grey paint was chipped off the one story wood framed house. They greeted me with a smile though and pointed me to an extra chair they had brought outside just for me. With such a nice welcome, I felt I owed them at least a little conversation.

I introduced myself, asked some standard questions to determine their investment objectives and then presented the Fidelity Trend Mutual Fund. I talked about the Fund's past performance, diversification, and various investment plans. The Rollins were a pleasant couple and asked surprisingly good questions. I talked for twenty minutes while they just smiled and nodded their heads before Mr. Rollins finally responded.

"Well Ma, what ya think?" Mr. Rollins said, looking over at his wife. "Seems like this young man knows what he's talking about."

"Sounds good to me," she answered. "Let's do it."

Now the tough part. I had to tell them about the $500 minimum, expecting that surely they were planning to invest a smaller amount.

Before I could utter the words, Mr. Rollins handed me a savings booklet from Citizens Bank and asked me to look at their balance. I did; it was $15, 278. I almost gasped for air. That might not seem like much money by today's standards, but it was a lot for a rookie broker in 1968.

"And, how much of this would you like to invest in Fidelity Trend, Mr. Rollins?

"All but the change," he said. "You put the $15,000 in the fund for us."

I quickly figured my commission in my head; 8% commission on $15,000 was about $1,200, half would be mine. Exactly my first month's salary draw. In disbelief, I calmly proceeded with the paperwork, executed the order without telling them that it was my first, thanked them, and was out the door.

One block away from the Rollins' home I had to pull over to the side of the road. There, all by myself in the dark, I let out with a very loud "Yahoo!" Then I raced home to give Terry a big hug and take a quiet peek at our beautiful kids sleeping in their bedroom.

Mr. Rollins referred me to one of his friends, who invested $5,000, and I opened several other new accounts from my Warwick member contacts. In my mind, I was on my way. I was going to be a wealthy stockbroker.

My enthusiasm for the stock market began to dampen in my second year, however. The market softened and new accounts were tough to come by. I also began to lose respect for my job when the office manager began to encourage account activity through pushing DuPont underwritten stocks. Regardless of whether I personally thought they would perform well, company underwritten new issues and secondary offerings generated higher commissions. Pushing commissions didn't sit well with my vision of being a professional advisor.

Impatiently realizing I was not on any kind of a path to business ownership as a stockbroker, I began looking again for a career. I thought I had found it: a Management Recruiter's franchise. Matching people with jobs seemed like an ideal calling for me. So, I made the move. What I didn't count on was a recessionary economy.

General Motors and all their suppliers were laying workers off.

For a management recruiter, the object is to find matches in a supply of job applicants and a supply of open positions. The problem was that the applicant stack was stacked high with people who wanted big salaries and the job pile was slim, filled mostly with jobs from employers who wanted to hire people willing to take a cut in pay. I sold the business, leaving myself deep in debt with just enough money for about two months rent on our apartment.

Not a problem. I quickly found a job as a dining room manager at a Sheraton hotel in Pittsburgh with a promise to move into management if I proved myself. Four months later, I was promoted to Assistant Manager at the Sheraton Metro Inn at the Detroit Metro Airport. Meanwhile, my family was growing; Jeff was four, Marty two, and Cherri a tiny baby.

The Detroit Sheraton Metro Inn was a 160-room property with a large lower level banquet room. The building was a two story U-shaped structure with a swimming pool in the middle. We booked 50 to 100 of the rooms nightly to airline flight crews. I continued to work long hours, promoting the business in hopes that success at the Detroit Metro would enhance my chances to someday become a manager.

One night in my third month, as I passed the front desk after returning from a review of the banquet room, the desk clerk got my attention.

"Mr. Lobdell," he said, "the driver is on his way to pick up Mr. Ewing at the airport." Laird Ewing, the owner of the hotel, often arrived for an unannounced visit. The desk clerk told me this with a concerned look on her face and I knew why. Douglas, our GM, was out in the courtyard with Marvin, the head bartender, having wine and dinner with two airline stewardesses. I immediately went out to the courtyard to warn them Mr. Ewing was on his way.

As I proceeded down the hall toward the courtyard I had some selfish thoughts. I was just beginning to make payments on my $4,000 debt left over from my failed recruiting business. I had a wife and three kids at home and I was desperate to accelerate my career. I made a conscious decision not to go to the courtyard to warn Douglas.

Ewing wore his dark brown hair smoothly trimmed on his 5' 10" slightly portly frame. He was always neatly dressed in a sport coat with a collared shirt but no tie. The story was that he'd inherited a lot of money and chose to invest it in Sheraton hotels. He always toured the kitchen, talking to the cooks as he passed through. He would inspect the walk-in cooler and freezer, examine the steaks and taste some of the food, always wanting to be perceived as a food expert. Needless to say, I knew where I needed to be when Ewing arrived.

I had second thoughts though as I entered the kitchen. Being disloyal to a manager, especially one who was my boss, was not usually my nature. I only paused for a moment though. I had already made my decision.

As it was told to me later, Ewing walked to the edge of the courtyard, paused to look at the scene playing itself out there, and turned and walked toward the kitchen. When he walked through the doorway, the first thing he saw was me on the cook line assisting one of the cooks.

"Mr. Ewing, good to see you." I reached across the line to shake his hand while pretending to be surprised. We chatted briefly and then he was off to check into his room. When I arrived to work early the next morning, Mr. Ewing informed me that Douglas had been fired and that I was the new GM of the Detroit Sheraton Metro Inn. I was holding back tears when, from my new office, I called Terry to tell her the news. On my GM salary I was able to pay off my Management Recruiter debts within a year.

Mr. Ewing was aggressively buying new properties. His next acquisition was another airport property, the 300-room Randolph House in Liverpool, New York, just outside of Syracuse. The name was changed to Sheraton and the property needed an experienced airport manager. I was transferred with one week's notice. We lived in the hotel for a month until we could find an apartment. Room service for every meal and an indoor pool was fun for the first week. After three weeks of that kind of life, we were happy to move into an apartment.

My new property was a convention hotel with a large banquet hall and five conference rooms. Thanks to an amazing sales director, we were able to increase sales by 35% in our first year as a Sheraton. Our sales director, Betty Hertz, was a fifty-year-old former Miss Pennsylvania contestant with a vivacious personality.

Betty frequently made the one hundred mile drive to the state capital, where she always stayed overnight. She spent a lot of money, but promised to return with at least one new booking. She always did. I wasn't sure I could believe all her stories, especially the one about knowing Governor Nelson Rockefeller whom she referred to as "Rocky." Then, one day she alerted everyone that Rocky was coming to our hotel. Sure enough, that day Nelson Rockefeller stepped out of his Limo, walked into our hotel and gave Betty a big hug.

Ewing hired a Director of Operations, Bill Stevens, and based him out of the Sheraton Syracuse. Stevens was able to help with hotel operations, enabling me to spend much of my time working with convention business. Stevens was more interested in socializing with Betty Hertz than managing the hotel. Fortunately, he was traveling most of the time. Ewing had made a deal with me that I would get 5% of the entire bar business, a deal that turned out to be very good for me. I was taking in an extra $1,000 a month in commissions. Once Ewing realized how my deal was working out, he needed to find a way out. I was making more money than his new director of operations. Ewing started talking about wanting to transfer me to a new hotel he was building in Pittsburgh.

Meanwhile, Terry and I got a surprise. She was pregnant for our fourth baby, and a few months later gave birth to a beautiful new son, Gregory Matthew. The next time I heard comments about my possibly being transferred to Pittsburgh, I began exploring options for yet another career change. I had several choices, two of which were back in Michigan, which Terry preferred.

A mailed resume and a phone interview resulted in an offer to pay travel expenses for me to come to Traverse City, Michigan to interview with a company called Franchise Foods International (FFI). I had never forgotten my favorable impression of Traverse City on my previous visit there to interview with directors of the Traverse City County Club. In fairness to Mr. Ewing, I gave my notice. Two weeks later I was on my way back to Michigan with Terry and our four little ones, all under six.

I gasped within at the offer they gave me. Just $12,000; less than half the $30,000 I had been making in New York. I countered with a request for a little more money, along with some ownership and an option to eventually buy in as partner. Hubbell and Purdom called me the next morning, generously meeting my request. My position was Operations Manager, reporting directly to Hubbell and Purdom.

My first task was to turn around a troubled restaurant in Manistee, sixty miles south of Traverse City. Apparently that was a test. Three months later I moved to Traverse City to take over as General Manager of FFI. This was the opportunity I had been striving years for. I was an equity partner, could call my own shots, and saw operations that could easily be brought to profitability.

Working eighty and ninety hour weeks and driving 50,000 miles a year, I had some locations remodeled, re-located others, and acquired additional locations as cash flow permitted. When I reached the point of becoming a full partner and the company was generating comfortable profits, the objectives of my partners and I began to differ. They wanted more benefits and larger draws. I wanted growth. The answer was to split. Subsequent to the resolution of the typical uncomfortable challenges of splitting partnerships, Terry and I became sole owners of four Kentucky Fried Chicken restaurants in Lobdell Management Company.

My long hours continued. I took some chances and had some luck. Well, maybe I could take some credit for assuming that the high inflation and high interest rates of the Jimmy Carter years would not continue. My side hobby was then, and continues to be, studying the economy and the American Presidency. My historical favorites are Washington, Lincoln, the Roosevelts, and Truman. I was a big fan of John and Bobby Kennedy, didn't care much for Lyndon Johnson, was appalled at Richard Nixon, found our own Michigan guy, Gerald Ford, acceptable, and then thought America was ready for "change" and supported Jimmy Carter in 1976.

I was wrong on that one, big time. We got "change" alright. But Carter's "change" ideas didn't work very well. The economy slowed, inflation went double digit, and interest rates soared.

Ironically, it worked out well for me. Businesses that were for sale in 1980 were cheap because sensible buyers didn't want to pay 20% interest. I probably wasn't being sensible at the time, but I became a converted economic conservative and bet that Reagan would revive the economy. My gamble paid off. I got some great prices on more KFC restaurants, financed with those absurd 20% floating interest rates, and was happy when the interest rates began dropping and the economy started improving under Reagan. I continued to work long hours and to expand throughout the early 1980s; ultimately enjoying the rewards of twelve KFC restaurants divided between northern Michigan and central Illinois.

Then in my mid forties, I decided the time had come to shift gears and enjoy more time with Terry and my teenage family. I sold the KFCs and commenced on a new path of diversification. I started a leasing company, opened some Ten Minute Oil Change shops and dabbled in some venture capital investments. My best new venture was a return to the food business with the opening of a Taco Bell restaurant in Traverse City. This time around, my plan was to bring in a partner. I found the right fit with the right guy at the right time.

With the help of a professional recruiter, I discovered Ken Underwood, an experienced restaurant operator seeking an equity opportunity to move to the Traverse City area. I provided the money for growth in the business and gave Ken some equity with the understanding that I would eventually shift my energies to other investment projects. We worked together long enough for me to become confident that his methods of operation were compatible with mine; gradually allowing me to reduce my involvement to simple consulting. As we eventually expanded operations into upstate New York, I added Steve Pinkerton from Syracuse as a partner and Director of Operations. Steve provided excellent leadership in adding partners, Lou DiFrancesco and Wahid Akl. Ken Underwood retired in 2009 and my son Marty joined me as partner and CEO. Our New York operations, as of 2010, are in Buffalo, Rochester, Syracuse, Albany and other surrounding communities.

Success in business is all about selecting and providing opportunity for good people. With the fortune of dedicated and skilled partners I have been able to diversify into other areas that interested me; most importantly investing in my son's businesses and establishing a family enterprise that we can all share in. Jeff, Marty, Cherri and Greg are partners with Terry and me in Lobdell Family Enterprises, a company with diversified investments in restaurants, real estate, money management, and gas and oil.

Thankful for our life in Traverse City, and the opportunities the restaurant business has provided, Terry and I have been able to do our share of giving back to local charities. One of our favorites of these experiences has been with Northwestern Michigan College (NMC), where Terry serves on the Foundation Board. In appreciation for our contributions, the NMC Great Lakes Culinary Institute named their teaching restaurant, "Lobdell's." We have a great time watching the students at work when we dine at Lobdell's for lunch and sponsor an annual scholarship dinner. In addition to that teaching restaurant, our sons own seven restaurants in Traverse City. Consequently, we have a lot of choices for dining. And the price is right.

At a 2008 NMC dinner, where Terry and I appreciated being honored as Fellows of NMC, I told a story about dining out at one of our son's restaurants. When asked by the waitress how it was that I was lucky enough to get a 100% discount card, I said, "I changed the owner's diapers." That got a laugh. A bigger laugh came though when Terry corrected me as to who really changed all those diapers.

Over the years, I have enjoyed and continue to enjoy the challenge of new ventures. Fortunately, I can consider all but one to have had some level of success. The failure, a drive thru only chicken take out in Chicago, ended as the result of a failed partnership. Others had varying levels of success; the Ten Minute Oil change did very well; I had moderate success with a Precision Tune Vehicle Maintenance franchise and a Sparkle Wash International pressure washing business.

One of my most enjoyable business experiences came in the designing, developing and operating of a miniature golf business in Indian Shores Florida. The project came as a part of a personal plan to experience some sunshine in the winter months in Florida. The day we opened Fiesta Falls in 1990, a Spanish castle theme concept with a four story high structure, waterfalls and a pirate ship simulated afloat in a river, was a blast---and a money maker to boot. It was a was a real kick to see this creation swarmed with family tourists scattered about the course under the bright lights, having fun on this creation that I had helped to design and where I spent many hours shoveling dirt and carving concrete into huge rocks. The business did well and I opened another in Watertown, New York. I sold the businesses in the late nineties to lighten my work load.

Like most venture capitalists, I have to admit I am drawn by the excitement of risk taking, but have kept my risk venture investments within the framework of what I feel I can afford to lose; that is where gas and oil speculation and horse racing has entered my life.

My gas and oil investments have been with a lifelong experienced developer from Traverse City, David Hall. In over fifteen years of investing I have had some wins and a few losses while enjoying the voyage. Our largest project has been a partnership venture under contract with the US Military to drill for natural gas at the Fort Knox military base in Louisville, Kentucky. This project called Red One, which we began discussing in 2006 and drilled our first well in 2009, involved a substantial investment which is providing modest returns so far, but was still a work in progress in 2011.

As for horse racing, this definitely rates as my highest risk venture; yet it is the business I most enjoy. I have fond memories of riding a horse bare back as child and have followed thoroughbred racing all my life. Now, I find buying and owning young thoroughbreds with famous bloodlines and dreaming of joining one of my horses in the winner's circle to be very inspiring. In September of 2010 I bought two yearling colts with impressive pedigrees; Dayne's Wonder (named after my grandson, Dayne and the sire, Stevie Wonderboy, who had been owned by the late Merv Griffin); and Niam's Strike (named after my grandson, Niam and sire, Smart Strike, one the great sires of the past twenty years). I provide updates on a website, lobdellstables.com.

In my view, all these projects are what free enterprise and entrepreneurship is all about. After years of having many 70-80 hour work weeks, then finally achieving enough financial independence to be able to risk digging for oil and racing horses, it occurs to me that I continue to enjoy my climb from the cellar. My family, my business partners, and my friends bring me joy most every day. It's a great country that we live in where, with hard work, smarts, and a little luck, a boy can rise to manhood in such away. God Bless America.

So, that's some highlights of how my life turned out. Here's what happened to the other people in my story.

Howard and Marion

My father, my mother, Gerald, and Lavern all faced a common challenge in their aging years: pessimism. All four of these people I loved and cared for dearly each felt a sense of pessimism about tomorrow after brooding about the obstacles and disappointments of yesterday and today.

I encouraged them to bury unpleasant thoughts of the past and concentrate on finding ways to see better days ahead. "Fix it yourself or find another person to help," was my motto in tough times. I tried to convince them that thinking of the needs of others would help them forget their own problems. I like to think my encouragement helped them at times. More often than not though, the challenge of depression took its toll.

My father, Howard, lived until he was 75, struggling in his last five years, his lungs eventually collapsing from the damage TB had done to him when he was in his forties. My mother, Marion, lived to 84. For the entire nine years she lived after Dad died, she said she was anxious to die to go to heaven and join him.

My parents had some good years after retiring. They took a long trip to Yellowstone National Park, vacationed at campgrounds, and enjoyed visits with Terry, me, and their grandchildren.

As my business grew and we built a nice home with a swimming pool, my father was extremely proud. He would always ask me, "How much you make an hour?" He wanted to tell his friends back home. I tried to explain to him that I didn't really know the amount I earned by the hour. "I will know when my accountant tells me at the end of the year," I told him.

"You don't know until the end of the year?" For the life of him he could not understand this concept. He pretended to understand, but a few months later he would size up our home, and our cars, and ask me again, always with pride in his voice, "How much you figure you make an hour?"

Like all grandparents, my mother and father enjoyed baby sitting their grandchildren and Terry and I took advantage of this on several occasions to attend conventions in Las Vegas and Hawaii. Our son, Jeff, recalls being in a car with his grandpa Lobdell hoping for a Detroit Tiger ninth inning rally to win a baseball game. My Dad insisted his grandsons all cross their fingers for the Tigers to win the game. As Jeff recalls, the Tigers still came up short. Somebody must have forgotten to keep their fingers crossed.

Reverend Friendly

From what I have told you so far about my oldest brother, Lavern, you would have to question his intelligence; in other words, from all outward appearances he would seem to be just plain stupid. Why else would someone put themselves in so many circumstances certain to turn out poorly? My family, however, would later find out that Lavern wasn't stupid at all, and was actually quite bright, but suffering from a probable brain disorder. Whatever his affliction, he was totally lacking in common sense, certainly. However, Lavern does have a great capacity to remember details and is a gifted sales person. He can write a long speech, memorize it, and then recite it – with passion – without so much as glancing at his notes. As an adult, his goal became making a living as a professional speaker.

Lavern's first gigs stirred up nothing but our family's embarrassment. He developed speeches about how he had saved himself as a sinner. How he was a drunk and forger of checks now reborn. In these speeches he talked about his days inside county jails across the country and finally even detailed his time in Jackson State Prison. His "days of sin were over," he said; he had found the Lord. As he fine-tuned it, the speech appealed to small groups on college campuses.

But the students would pay him and then invite him out to drink. The next thing you knew, he was plastered and was soon a different person than the man who'd just delivered the inspiring speech. From there the evening usually ended with Lavern disturbing the peace and back in jail. He could talk though, and he never stayed in those small town jails very long. He was always able to convince some judge that he had learned his lesson and would start fresh, following the straight and narrow path of a preacher.

At some point in his forties, Lavern became interested in philosophy: in particular, the works of Kahlil Gibran, a Lebanese American artist, poet, and writer. Gibran is ranked close to Shakespeare as one of the best selling poets in history. Lavern memorized Gibran's poetry and he could recite it nonstop for an hour or more without

189

missing a word. In addition to his study of Gibran, Lavern also read and studied the Bhagavada Gita, one of the three holiest scriptures of Hinduism. He recites the Gita for hours at a time. With the help of a friend, Lavern wrote a hundred pages of what he calls, "the American interpretation" of the Gita.

This new poetry reciting soon became a better gig than the "ex-con" speech. Lavern spoke to student groups at Marquette University, the University of Detroit, Wayne State, and other colleges. He was on track to making a good living doing what he loved to do, but somehow that track always became muddy. Money for him was like rain on a dirt road – whenever he had any a big mess was sure to come, and come soon.

At the end of every speech, there were always new friends who wanted to party. After a night of drinking, the students could stagger back to their dorms but Lavern would wander the streets, his behavior out of control, and would ultimately end up in jail. As he grew older, his alcoholism evolved into drinking sprees that kept him busy entering and exiting rehab centers. A master at convincing judges and counselors that he had learned his lesson and would never drink again, his cycles of indulgence and recovery became a way of life for Lavern.

When my father died, his lungs finally collapsing, Lavern was in the Muskegon County Jail. The Muskegon police escorted him from his cell to the funeral and then back to jail. A policeman stood at the back of the funeral service while Lavern sat between my mother and me. I escorted him to Dad's open casket, and looked out at my older brother while I delivered the eulogy. Giant tears rolled down his cheeks. I believe he was saying to himself how sorry he was for all the trouble he had caused.

By the time my mother passed away, Lavern had moved to Colorado, prohibited as he was from entering Muskegon County. The Muskegon police had told Lavern to leave town, and that if he ever returned they would send him back to Jackson Prison for ten years. He took their advice and has not only stayed out of their county, but has never returned to Michigan.

When my mother died, I made a half-days worth of phone calls to alcohol rehab centers in Colorado, trying to locate Lavern. I found him at a center in Boulder. He was saddened by our mother's death, but acted somewhat pleased when I let him know that I had told our mother a white lie in her final days; that Lavern was healthy, sober, and doing well in Colorado.

The Denver-Boulder, Colorado area has been Lavern's home since the mid-eighties. Gerald had long ago reached a point where he refused to talk to Lavern and so since our parents have passed on, I'm the only remaining family member for Lavern to talk to.

His life has been a vicious repeating cycle. He goes into rehab, talks them into a release, they locate a state subsidized apartment for him, he collects SSI payments, and I send him a weekly check. Lavern tells me how great he is doing and gives me his new phone number. I call periodically to check on him. Three to six weeks later, the phone is disconnected and I can't locate him.

Eventually, I get a collect call from him at my office. "I know you have heard this before, but I am going to stop drinking for good this time," he always says. The only person who would have believed him, and believed him every time without fail, would have been my mother. This cycle has occurred about five times a year for more than ten years. Once, he was picked up off the street for dead, only to be determined to be still alive and sent to a hospital.

Lavern is always thankful for my phone calls and has pleaded with me for years to come to see him. In the spring of 2007, I told him that I would fly to Colorado for a visit if he would stay sober for six months. He promised that he would. With one month to go, I bought a plane ticket to Denver. Ten days before my trip, I called to give him my travel details only to find him at the other end of the line, plastered drunk. I prepared to cancel my flight but then, true to form, he called me the next day, begging for forgiveness and so I made the trip. I found Lavern in good health, sober, and shedding happy tears when he met me at the airport.

When he's sober, my brother does well in his life in Colorado; in his speaking engagements he bills himself as, "Reverend Friendly." Sporting a long white beard, a rugged face from his back alley life, and slightly smaller than his original 5' 7" frame, Lavern limps along through downtown Boulder, looking for people who know him. And he is, in fact, frequently addressed by those who have heard him rattle off poetry on a corner, or who have picked him up off the street at one time or another. His circle of acquaintances ranges from the homeless to the street venders and merchants, to the Boulder police and workers from the alcohol rehab centers. They all greet him as Reverend Friendly.

Somehow, Lavern has come under the protection of a woman named Kim. A wonderful lady, Kim has been staying with Lavern in his Boulder apartment for two years now, as of this writing. Kim is the best thing that has happened to Lavern since he left home fifty seven years ago. This is the first time he has been in an apartment for more than a year. He's now 74; considering how he's treated his body, it's amazing that he's still alive.

Kim is a pleasant and tiny little lady, likely in her fifties. She moves about in her short cropped hair and slim body with lots of nervous energy. Kim is a firm advocate of herbs and vitamins and is a very caring person, especially towards Lavern. She encourages him to eat healthy meals and stay away from alcohol. If, however, Lavern chooses to drink again she is powerless to stop him.

I made a return visit to see my brother in May of 2008. On this trip I decided to really talk to him about his life, so I'd come back with a better understanding of how he and I had turned out so differently. What I found was that tracking Lavern's troubled path with any degree of accuracy was simply not feasible. His own recollections are scattered and inconsistent. The jails and detox centers he has occupied throughout the country are too numerous to count. The only regular job he ever had was selling magazines; eventually though, he ran out of magazine companies that hadn't heard of his alcohol related escapades and so he found temporary homes in Chicago, Los Angeles, Philadelphia, and many other cities across the U.S. The city police departments would soon get to know him and, with the threat of jail time hanging over his head, he'd leave town. Sometimes the police departments even bought his bus ticket.

On this latest visit, I interviewed him for hours while he was sober, and later I even questioned the police, the social workers, and the social service volunteers who have had to deal with him over the years. I was especially interested in the details of him being committed to a mental hospital in Denver a few years earlier, an attempt by Denver authorities to keep him off the streets.

I had recalled the phone call he made to me in Michigan on a Friday night, telling me of his plight. "You gotta get me out of here.

This place is for people who have lost their mind, gone whacko. I'm not a whacko. Get me out of here," he had pleaded. I remember trying to call the hospital office, but being told I would have to call back Monday morning. When I made the Monday call I was told that Lavern had "mysteriously escaped."

Now talking with Lavern in Colorado, Lavern filled me in on the details of his adventure:

With the help of several other patients, Lavern gathered up a dozen sheets and tied them together into a long rope. He broke the lock on a window in his room and tied one end of this "sheet rope" to his bedpost and dropped the other end out the window, and it trailed down three stories to the ground. While a collaborating patient distracted the floor guard, Lavern used the knots he'd tied in the sheets to grasp with his hands and, bracing his feet against the brick wall, he scaled down the outside of the building to freedom. This all happened under the cover of darkness, at about one in the morning.

"I gave those nuts the best show they'd ever seen!" he exclaimed to me proudly.

Chilled and without a jacket, Lavern somehow made his way to the Denver bus station where he spent the night curled up in a chair. With only a few dollars in his pocket, he bought a bottle of cheap wine and the cheapest ticket to the next town, which turned out to be Boulder. His memory of where he went and how long he survived in Boulder is blank. Lavern's next recollection is waking up at the Boulder Drug and Alcohol Rehab Programs and Addiction Treatment Center.

An expert on alcohol treatment centers as a result of his firsthand experience, Lavern considers the Boulder center to be the best. Subsequent to drying out, counseling, and amusing the staff with his poetry, Lavern was released and provided an apartment. The only hitch was the required $600 deposit. He met that requirement with a call to me in Michigan. I also obtained a phone for him and started sending him weekly spending money checks.

Two months later one of my weekly calls was met with a "phone disconnected," message. He was back in detox. This cycle of detox, release to an apartment with another deposit, and ultimately back to detox continued in Boulder for several years.

One interruption of his routine came about with Lavern's

discovery of a new dwelling. The way Lavern tells it, just prior to dawn one morning, with cash in his pocket accumulated from several of the weekly checks I had sent him, Lavern slipped out a back door of the treatment center. He walked to a bicycle shop where he bought a used bike and backpack filled with supplies. He was off to the nearby Rocky Mountains.

Thirty miles from town, a downpour, thunder and some smacks of lightning prompted my brother to seek cover. He dragged himself and his bike into some bushes. By the time the storm had subsided, darkness was only a couple hours away and he needed better cover for the night. A mile and half back down the mountain, he found it. A large rock cave. The cave was composed of two parts, an entry fifteen feet in width by six feet in depth and twenty feet high. Beyond that was a two foot by four foot opening leading into a six by eight space with a five foot ceiling. Lavern had not only found cover for the night, he had found a new home – for a while, anyway.

His backpack was filled with canned fruits and vegetables, a little dried fruit, and some books. Combined with matches to light a fire, water from a nearby stream, and some marijuana he'd scored somehow, almost all his needs were met. Within a few days though, lonesome and running low on supplies, Lavern ventured back to his bike. He pedaled seven miles down the highway to a country store where he purchased more canned fruits and vegetables, oatmeal, and replaced a lost toothbrush.

The cave became his home for three weeks, his only human contact some passing hikers whom he amused with his philosophy recitals. I'm sure the hikers had an interesting story to tell their friends about their hiking confrontation with a cave-man philosopher.

Finally, out of money and thirsty, Lavern returned to Boulder where he bought a bottle of rubbing alcohol to satisfy his craving. The next morning he was picked up off the street again for a return to the detox center. A couple weeks of rehab and a call to me resulted in another apartment. The cave, however, was not forgotten. He returned many times for stays ranging from a few days to two weeks. He claimed he got a " spiritual boost" from his trips to the cave.

The security aspect of his environment never fazed him; at least not until the day his presence was challenged when he returned from a walk. He heard movement in the brush behind him and thought that something or someone was following him. Glancing back over his shoulder, he spotted a large cat, probably a cougar. At that moment he told me that he thought of Carlos Castaneda's writings about Don Juan. Carlos, on a hike with Don Juan, had seen some type of cat moving toward them. Carlos had abruptly decided that he and Don Juan should make a run for it.

"Running is the last thing we want to do," advised Don Juan. Juan explained that animal predators sense fear quickly, encouraging them to attack. With this in mind, Lavern was determined to appear confident, fearless, and to ignore his predator. He stopped at a tree, leaned against it, slid down and placed his body in a half lotus position and avoided looking at the cat. Hearing the cat move closer, he proceeded to light a marijuana cigarette. He smoked away, he said, feeling calmness in his breath while the cat stopped and stared at him. Two hours later, and half asleep, Lavern rose to find that the cat had disappeared

Despite my exhaustive interviews with my brother and the people who now know him best, I still don't have the expertise to make a medical judgment; I can only conclude that he is probably bipolar. Most certainly he is a severe and chronic alcoholic. Maybe my father had it right all those years ago when he said, "Lavern was never right after that accident at Louie Sternburg's farm." As of this writing he as been sober for more than a year, his longest sober period in nearly sixty years. Thank God for Kim who is still with him.

A Name from the Past

Rebecca Mills is not sure of her birth date. She never lived in a basement like Gerald and me, but rather spent her early childhood somewhere much less desirable; a children's home. Rebecca's birth certificate reads "Baby Girl Brown," the daughter of birth mother, Nancy Lee Brown. She was adopted out as Rebecca Segelstrom in 1969.

When asked about her life, Rebecca said she only wants to remember her early years on a small farm and her current life on a small piece of land with some chickens and pigs.

"My fondest memories," Rebecca tells me, "were of a foster home—a farm up in Fremont. I thought I'd grow up there and was quite content with these people. It felt like home, and I never thought of leaving. Unfortunately, my case worker arrived one day. I recognized her immediately and hid in the barn. That poor woman suffered my protest all the way to her car."

"I hated the city. There were no animals in their barns that they called garages, only a spider in a dusty side window. Their yards were small, with fences that blocked away silent, foreboding strangers on the other side. The good Lord did give me an ounce of comfort, though. There was a small cherry tree that grew out back. It gave me branches to hide in and taught me patience while I waited for its small fruits to ripen. I still yearn for those wide open fields of Johnson grass though. That old cliché about taking a child out of the country must be true, for it never left me."

When I sought her out, Rebecca was willing to talk to me about one especially important day in her adult life. Curious about her birth parents, she began asking questions and kept asking them for years before locating her birth mother, Nancy Lee Brown. Brown didn't have much interest in talking to Rebecca, but did give her the name of her birth father, my brother, Gerald Lobdell.

When she happened to mention this name to a friend, the friend told her that a man by that name lived nearby. She drove to the man's house and parked. She saw that he had some items for sale in his front yard. Besides being a good woodworker, Gerald was mathematically and mechanically inclined and was always able to do his own plumbing, repair his own cars and cycles. He was a shrewd buyer, always getting a deal on cars, motor homes, ATVs, and lawn mowers. When he didn't need something anymore he would usually be able to sell it for more than he paid for it. Sometimes by putting it in the yard.

Rebecca got out of her car and admired the man's sturdy work on a picnic table. What Rebecca didn't know at the time was that the man she was looking at learned how to build sturdy things from my father, her grandfather, Howard Lobdell. At my request Rebecca described the incident to me:

"I recall admiring a wooden bench swing and a picnic table," she said. "When he emerged from his house, he asked whether I was interested in purchasing it, giving me no other choice but to reveal my true purpose for being there. 'Are you Gerald Lobdell?' I asked nervously, searching his face for any reaction. 'Yeah,' he replied, with a rather bewildered look.

"'Rebecca,' I said as I presented a hand shake. 'Nice to meet you.' I could see tension rising as he grew somewhat leery of me. 'Do you recall a girl, years ago, by the name of Nancy Brown?'

"His face produced a fearful look of dread, and he took a defensive step back in retreat. 'My, my wife,' he stuttered, as he pointed back, 'Is right in the house.' I put up my hand in a surrendering motion, hoping to calm his fears. 'Do you remember that baby she had?' He began to make several steps back toward the house. 'I'm that baby,' I quickly added before he had the chance to leave and forever withhold any response. 'Please don't go away. Please. I just want to know you better. This might be the last I ever see of you, and I've wondered about you my whole life. Please talk to me, even if it's just for a little while.'

"To my surprise, he did indeed stop. He asked where I lived, so that he might meet me there later. There was a long awkward silence as we both studied each other's faces. It didn't take me long to see who I took after. This is where I got my dark hair and olive complexion, I recall thinking. In one sense, I didn't want to leave, for I feared a permanent dismissal. But in consideration of him, I knew I couldn't stay. The people in that house were obviously an obstacle to any hope of reception.

"Back home, my dad – your brother – arrived a few hours later. I could see a sense of delightful surprise in his face as he looked around at my children.

"I'm a grandfather?" he inquired.

"Yes you are, if that's okay with you. This is Michael, this is Kari, this is Matthew, and the youngest here is Brandon.' He smiled and talked to them a minute."

That evening, Gerald called me at my home in Traverse City. He reminded me of the incident that occurred some twenty-seven years earlier; the incident in which he had to go to court and was held financially responsible for costs connected with the birth of Nancy Lee Brown's baby. I remembered the day clearly because I had just returned home from Ferris State College to help and support him.

"She's normal," he exclaimed of Rebecca. "She's a nice-looking girl, and her kids are all nice looking and normal."

"Why wouldn't they be? " I said out loud, though I knew the meaning of his statement. He had this idea in his head that he didn't want to have kids because they might inherit his learning disability. I could never convince him that he was fine, only burdened with some limitations on reading and writing because of the damage done by rheumatic fever, and because of his limited education.

Gerald worked for thirty years at Johnson's Products, mostly as a fork lift driver. He finally married at the age of 42 to a 27-year-old Native American woman, Cindy. With my busy life of long working hours, moving, and struggling to find time for my family, I found less time to see Gerald over the years.

He would become angry at me for what he considered my neglect and resented the time I spent with Terry's family. Terry had a big family, including lots of little cousins our own kid's ages. So, that was where we went when we came to town. I would usually try to stop and see Gerald for a short visit on our way into town.

Gerald and Cindy both drank heavily and Gerald would even mix alcohol with the prescription drugs he took for depression. They never had any children and Cindy didn't want anything to do with Rebecca. Gerald's love for and interest in his daughter contributed to his escalating conflict with Cindy and they eventually divorced.

All our later years were not as stressful as those disagreements, though. We took some trips back to our old farm, asked the owners for a tour of the house, and walked together through the woods that we had played cowboys and indians in as boys. We looked where we had built the hay fort in the barn, talked about Big Buster the bull, our trips to the Ravenna Fair, and the skirmishes with Wally Wagoner.

One night I got a frantic phone call from a cousin, who said he just heard on the news that Gerald's house burned and he had been pulled from the fire. I called the hospital and prepared to drive to Muskegon. The hospital informed me that he was not injured seriously and would be released soon. I called later that evening. He seemed physically intact but obviously very upset about his home and I invited him to come stay with Terry and me. Gerald said he preferred to stay with a friend so that he could be near his home to first deal with the insurance, and then re-build.

A police and fire department report, implying possible negligence, caused the insurance company to reject Gerald's claim. I offered to help him hire an attorney, but he didn't want my advice. Instead, he went to the police and fire departments and argued with them about their report. Some of the information it contained had been obtained from neighbors and his ex wife, all of whom he had been feuding with. His misguided and confrontational approach resulted in a two-year delay of his claim and the eventual settlement was only a fraction of what his home had been worth.

Rather than rebuild, Gerald chose to sell his lot and the remnants of his burned down house. I offered to help him purchase another home but he became angry with me at the suggestion that he would take charity. In a new scaled down lifestyle, Gerald purchased a house trailer and moved to a trailer park.

"Uncle Gerald has drowned in Lake Michigan," were the frightful words I heard my son say to me on the phone on the hot summer Wednesday, July 19, 2006.

Minutes after gasping for air at the horrible news, I slumped into a chair and remembered Gerald and me dog paddling in the muddy waters of Crockery Creek. I had an image of him and me, in happier times, alone with the turtles, bloodsuckers, and debris.

"Why wasn't I there to help him?" I thought to myself, remembering the time that I tackled him away from the electric fence that surrounded those muddy waters we had played in together more than fifty years ago.

Having digested the shock, I finally broke down and cried in the passenger seat of our car as Terry drove us to Muskegon. "Why couldn't I make him understand that I wanted to help him? Why couldn't I reach him?" I was thinking of the many times in recent years that he became angry at me for reasons unknown.

Terry told me that I had done my best. I gathered my thoughts and remembered the last piece of advice I had given Gerald; bury past difficulties and try to look toward a better day tomorrow. When we arrived in Muskegon, the details of Gerald's death came to light.

Michigan had sustained a severe hot spell in the summer of 2006. Gerald had been sharing his trailer with a cousin, Will Ziarnko. Will, my mother's sister Evelyn's son, was unemployed and needed a place to stay. Just like our father, Gerald could not turn down a person in need. Will helped with some of Gerald's expenses and kept him company. Sometimes Will's younger sister, Starla, would stop by for a visit and she soon became Gerald's best friend.

Starla is a loving and friendly person; she is also a good listener. Gerald had a lot of anger in his later years and needed someone to let off steam to; Starla had more patience than I or almost anyone else for Gerald's tirades against his doctor, the police, the fire department and sometimes me, for neglecting him.

In the hot days of that summer, Gerald was cooling off from the heat, certainly, but probably also from his own anger, by swimming in nearby Lake Michigan. On the day he drowned, some teenagers reported seeing an elderly man dog paddling about 100 yards off shore, headed for a sand bar.

The waves and undercurrent can be strong and unpredictable along the Lake Michigan shoreline. A beach walker and her son discovered Gerald's body washing ashore. The beach walker tried artificial respiration but was unsuccessful and ran to the nearest phone to call 911. Gerald was pronounced dead on the scene by an emergency rescue squad.

Terry and my children, Jeff, Marty, Greg, and Cherri, all participated with me in giving a eulogy for Gerald. Many friends, fellow workers, and relatives helped us with his farewell. We placed him at rest next to my father and mother.

A New Lobdell Generation

I have been blessed. With career success yes; but even more with family. All my hours of work took me away from our home often, and so Terry took it upon herself to take charge of the obligations at home, and what a fabulous wife and Mom she is! She has the talent to pursue a career of her own and could have been successful at whatever she chose.

Terry taught school to supplement our income in the early years of our marriage, and then made a decision that I am forever thankful for – to stay home with our children. Terry also supported me in every decision that I made in advancing my career even when it involved moving, changing jobs, traveling, taking risks, and working long into the night and over many weekends. From the days of junior high school when I was looked on as a bum by teachers, through the business or investment failures, she always had confidence in me that I would find a way to succeed. As I see it today, this ever-positive attitude that Terry has is responsible for the current success, positive attitudes, and happiness of our three sons and our daughter. It helped me succeed, too.

I tried to help her at home whenever I could. Often, while working late, I would dash home to help with baths for the kids and tucking them into bed. My favorite tuck-in game was to take on a make believe character that I called "Hilly Pilly." Hilly would only come if they were good and went to bed quietly. Hilly would suddenly appear in their room wearing a sport coat with about six ties on, wearing two different shoes and missing one sock. Worst of all, he would usually forget to put on his pants. He had a baggy hat, dark glasses pushed down on his nose, a make-believe mustache and a goatee from a black pencil. His ears were pinned back with tape and his front teeth protruded over his lower lip when he talked.

Hilly would announce, "Hi, I'm Hilly Pilly. I'm a really cool guy. I'm really good at doing stuff. Watch me catch the ball," he would proclaim as he took a ball from his pocket and tossed it in the air. The ball would slip through his hands and drop to the floor. Jeff, Marty, Cherri, and Greg (ages two to seven) would all laugh.

Next, Hilly would take off his tie to show the kids, only to realize he still had another one on, and another one, and so on. The kids would call to his attention that he had one sock on and different shoes. Finally, they would all say "Hilly, you forgot your pants." Hilly wouldn't look down at first. He would only say, "No, you guys are silly. I wouldn't forget my pants."

After repeatedly informing Hilly of his missing pants, he would finally slowly look down and realize the kids were right. He was only wearing jockey shorts. He would say, "Oh no, oh no, I did forget my pants," as he put his hands in front of himself and dashed out the door. I must have done the same silly routine a hundred times, including the times I did it for visiting little cousins; each time amusing my audience to ecstatic laughter. These days, my grandkids sometimes get a visit from Hilly Pilly.

My Hilly Pilly acting performance eventually lost its appeal after 1980 as the kids approached their teens. Then one day in the summer of 1994 I was personally touched with a reminder of what Hilly Pilly meant to them as kids. At a planned golf match with the boys, Jeff, Marty and Greg came to the match with a huge trophy which they had labeled as the Hilly Pilly Cup. In the summer of 2009 we will play our fifteenth annual Hilly Pilly Cup match. The teams are Jeff and I, MSU, vs. Marty and Greg, Michigan. We try to select a different unique golf course around the country for our match each year. I will only give you a hint as to who is leading: My occasional attempt at humor is to say we got two of our kids into MSU, but had to send the other two to Michigan because they couldn't get into MSU. Actually Terry and I are fans of both schools.

I never encouraged our kids to plan a career in the restaurant business; I wanted them to choose their path for themselves. Initially, Jeff, our oldest, was the only one interested in what has since become the family business. We did want to teach all of our kids the importance of the responsibility of work, though, regardless of what profession they chose. In practice, the amount they each worked became a little less with each child and was impacted by extra curricular activities. Jeff worked a lot while in high school,

Marty a little less, Cherri very little, and Greg was so busy with sports camps he didn't have time for any jobs.

Jeff, a high school hockey star and soccer player was a good student. He graduated from Michigan State University (MSU) and moved on to a career in the restaurant business. He had learned every phase of the business by the time he graduated from the same MSU restaurant management program that I had graduated from. Jeff spent five years in management with good companies before going into business for himself. He now owns fifteen restaurants and serves on the board of the Michigan Restaurant Association where he was Chairman in 2007. He is the best restaurant operator I have ever known in the business, myself included. Jeff has two sons, Dayne and Deacon, with wife Athena.

Our next son, Marty, showed early talents in both math and athletics. He came home from school in fifth grade with a message that he had scored the highest on a class math test. His teacher requested that we take him to a Northern Michigan math competition in Gaylord, 50 miles away. We went almost on a whim and Marty finished third among more than 250 kids. Two weeks later, I took him to the statewide competition in Ann Arbor where he finished above the two who were ahead of him in Gaylord, and was named one of Michigan's top twenty-five fifth grade math students.

Marty was also an avid sports fan at a very early age. He followed the Detroit Tiger baseball team and Lions football team with enthusiasm. While the boys were young, I didn't encourage them to play football even though I was a close follower of the Traverse City Trojans, the high school team, and attended all of their games. I just didn't expect my sons to be big enough to play high school football; especially not at a high school of 2,500 students that was annually ranked among the top ten teams in the state.

My hesitancy meant little to Marty though, and he decided that he wanted be a Trojan football player. He worked at it hard, lifting weights and sprinting. He played often as a junior, starting in several games. As a senior, Marty started every game, was a team captain and helped his team win the 1985 State Championship at the Pontiac Silver Dome, where the Detroit Lions played. Marty also became Co-Captain of his high school hockey team, played soccer and baseball, and ran the 880 in track. Marty was an honor student in high school as well as college and graduated from the University of Michigan with a B.A., a J.D. and an MBA. He spent the first fifteen years of his career in San Francisco where he practiced venture capital law, investment banking and was an executive for two technology companies, one of which he helped grow from a start-up to a successful public company. Eventually, he partnered with me in a fund of hedge funds fund, Lobdell Capital Partners (which ultimately merged with a NYC-based hedge fund, New Legacy).

Over the years, Lobdell family members often speculated when Marty might decide to settle down and get married. He seemed to be waiting for a magic bell to ring. In September of 2009, Marty decided to leave San Francisco and accept my offer to become my partner and assume the role of CEO of Hospitality Restaurant Group and Lobdell Management. I was excited with this development of Marty becoming my partner. The entire Lobdell family became excited about a development that occurred a few months after Marty moved to Michigan. Marty met Molly Medon, a beautiful and charming young management professional with Daimler-Mercedes Benz. That magic bell did finally ring, loud and clear. On December 30th, 2010, Marty proposed to Molly on Main Street in Ann Arbor, MI and they soon set a date of Sept 3rd, 2011 to commit their relationship for life.

"It's a girl!" Our third child was a daughter, Cherri, and what a thrill for Terry and me. With all the sports going on around our house, Cherri jumped in when she could, once having her nose broken when hit by a baseball. She ran track and played softball and did well at both. She also earned a coveted spot on the high school cheer leading squad. Sports, though, were not really her most important interest; she did it mostly to keep up with the family's sports enthusiasm. Cherri has a beautiful soprano voice and played the lead role as Marion the Librarian in the Traverse City High School Musical. Cherri also won the talent competition, singing a medley from Phantom of the Opera, and was first runner-up in the Miss Grand Traverse competition.

An excellent student, choosing the same school as her brother Jeff and her mom and dad, Cherri obtained her undergrad degree from Michigan State University and then went on for her

MBA from Northwestern University. Cherri was on her way to a successful career in creative advertising when she met and married a Northwestern classmate, Sanjay Malkani. They have three of our grandchildren, Niam, Ari, and Rowan.

Cherri, who urged me to write this book, is an active member of her church in Indianapolis, Indiana, and has become an inspirational leader to our family. She is a bright and talented lady who, like her Mom, could have excelled in a career of her choice. Instead, like her Mom, she chooses to devote her talent and energy to her three wonderful children.

"You may visit your wife in the third room down the hall," a nurse at the Syracuse, New York hospital instructed me. "She is beginning her labor."

"Labor? But she has our babies right away. We have never had a wait," I responded. At this point I am recalling the births of our other three. I just brought Terry to the hospital and by the time I finished the checking in paper work and found her room she had given birth.

"Sir, your wife is doing just fine."

"Have you called her doctor?"

"Sir, I will know when to call the doctor, that's my job. Your job is to help keep her calm."

"I think you should call now," I said as I walked away toward the room.

"I am ready to have the baby now," Terry grimaced as I entered the room.

Our fourth baby had not been in the plan. The year was 1970, the month, June. Cherri, at eighteen months was in diapers; not quite four-year-old Marty was not yet fully potty trained, and Jeff, our oldest, wasn't even six. We were living in Liverpool, New York, a suburb of Syracuse where I was managing the Sheraton Syracuse.

"Nurse, I need you to call our doctor now and my wife needs help. She is having a baby."

"Sir, you will have to calm down or you cannot be here," a lady who appeared to be in charge addressed me sternly. While I was being scolded one of the nurses headed toward Terry's room.

A couple minutes later the nurse who had entered Terry's room was wheeling her out. Other nurses gathered around to help. Terry was beginning to give birth while being wheeled to the delivery room. They still had not called the doctor. I wanted to whack somebody, but I remained calm. I just wanted Terry and the new baby to be OK.

Everything went fine. An intern delivered Gregory Matthew Lobdell. Terry was great and the joy of a beautiful new baby soon trumped my frustration with the maternity ward nurse.

If Cherri had it tough being the only girl, Greg didn't have it much easier, being three and half years younger than Marty and five and half years younger than Jeff.

Although very close to his big sister, Greg was more interested in sports than the opera. Chatting at his bedside after a fifth grade touch football game, Greg told me that he liked playing "QB." His eyes lit up when I told him he could someday be the quarterback of the Traverse City Trojan football team. Being QB for the Trojans became his goal that day, and I committed to help him; including running pass patterns in the back yard night after night.

As a proud father I could go on and on about our kid's many achievements. I could boast about Jeff's hat trick and MVP in a hockey tournament, Marty's big interception at the state championship football game or Cherri's musical performances. But, I will just give you one, Greg's 1988 State Championship football game; one of our last major family high school sporting events that also became a community affair. We organized a windsock relay from Traverse City to the Pontiac Silverdome, then home of the Detroit Lions, about ten marathons away.

A family friend, Ene Ripper, brought a large homemade windsock to our house as a gift to Greg, the team quarterback, as Traverse City's undefeated Trojan Class A high school football team prepared to play the Detroit Catholic Central Shamrocks.

I took a week off from work to plan the relay event, driving slowly to Pontiac and back. I mapped out the various points along the 250 mile route where runners would meet to pass off the windsock, carefully estimating times based on distances and speed of the runners. Fifty enthusiastic men and women participants of all ages joined our family on the relay team, taking distances from one mile to fifteen miles each.

The relay began in darkness early Thanksgiving morning and

arrived at game time Saturday at noon. Someone had said "The last one out of Traverse City turn out the lights" on Saturday as 30,000 Traverse City area fans watched the game, including a big standing ovation for the windsock as a cheerleader brought it onto the field. The Trojans won the game 24-14 to complete an undefeated season. Traverse City lights were turned back on in grand fashion that night as fire trucks and police cars escorted the champions the last five miles into town at midnight.

Greg was also first team All State in hockey and a sprinter and high jumper on the track team. He turned down a full ride scholarship offer to play football at Hillsdale College to try out as a walk on at the University of Michigan. Before the season began he decided that he was not likely to see playing time. He gave up football to concentrate on his education. Other than intramural sports, his football career was left for good memories.

Terry and I value educations and all our children were good students. Greg was an A student in high school and graduated from the University of Michigan with an undergrad degree in design and a postgraduate degree in architecture. He worked as an architect in San Francisco for five years and obtained his masters in management from Columbia University before joining his long time friend, Jon Carlson, in real estate development. Greg is married to his wonderful wife, Andi, and together they have another of our granddaughters, Jolie. They live in Ann Arbor, Michigan.

Today

I turned 68 years old on March 22, 2009. I have had the diverse experiences of many career challenges, but my primary career path and business focus for close to fifty years now, as of the writing of this book, has involved restaurants. While those experiences included all segments of the hospitality industry, Yum Brands (Taco Bell, KFC, Pizza Hut) franchises have provided the best opportunities for me. I visualize that relationship continuing for the remainder of my working days and then, hopefully, extending far into the future for my family.

I have fun every day keeping in touch with business investments, spending time with Terry, keeping in touch with my children and my grandchildren, following the ups and downs of our economy, and regularly reading about and discussing politics. Terry and I are seeing the world, and making new friends. I run three miles every other day, eat a healthy diet, read part of a book every day, and just plain enjoy my life. I fully expect to have many more business deals and family fun to look forward to in the years to come.

I try to live each day to the fullest, mixing family time with both work and my favorite hobbies of golf and reading about American history and the economy. My favorite forum for discussing these last two topics is Scuttlebutt. That's the name for a group of men I get together with every Thursday when I'm in Boca Raton. We exchange thoughts on a variety of issues on the government and the economy. These fifty men are almost all business and professional leaders; some like me are in Florida seasonally, and others are full time residents.

Most in the group are retired, including an economist, a New York City business consultant, CEOs, major real estate developers, money managers, doctors and attorneys. Because I'm an avid reader of history of the American Presidency, I am often asked to comment. Although I consider myself a lightweight among this bright group of men, I enjoy the challenge.

As I discuss these issues, I have concerns for my family's future and our succeeding generations. The world is becoming increasingly smaller and more interactive, economically and in political awareness. In my opinion, for America to remain vibrant and strong, we need to retain more of the traditional values we were founded on and place more emphasis on trying to balance our budgets, personally and in government. Meaningful debate is a part of our landscape, but too much time is spent on non-productive partisan battles and political posturing. Business, labor and government need to place more emphasis on integrity and accountability. The type of pride and loyalty we seek in our families should extend to our work and our country.

I have done some local work on Presidential campaigns, some Democrats and some Republicans. Once the election is over though I find my self pulling for the new President, regardless of party affiliation. I happen to believe that the founding fathers of this nation did a miraculous job in creating one of the greatest nations in the history of mankind. They were not perfect, but the system of government they created has allowed us to survive many wars, three depressions, financial market collapses and other disasters; all the while providing plenty of opportunities for Americans to climb their way to a better life.

I have made the climb from birth in a cellar, to living off the land on a small farm, and then surviving the rough streets of the Muskegon 'hood', narrowly escaping trouble. While making my climb I made money mucking out stalls, doing every type of farm chore, setting pins in a bowing alley, shoveling snow, cutting lawns, working on a factory assembly line, chauffeuring, and just about every type of job in the hospitality industry; each time doing the best I could, regardless of my job level or how tough my boss was. At the urging of my 14-year-old cheerleader girlfriend, and with memories of my hard-working father, I shifted onto a path seeking a better life. I hope this book can inspire some young readers to seek their own goal-oriented path in life.

I benefited from a great education at Michigan State University, aggressively pursued my career and from some great work experiences in management of a country club, restaurants, hotels, and even some time as a stockbroker, I found my way into business. After many long hours of work, risk-taking and associations with good people, I built a successful business development organization for my family. I've owned more than one hundred restaurants, a dozen auto service businesses, two miniature golf courses, a mutual fund trading system, numerous venture capital investments, various real estate, thoroughbred racehorses, and gas and oil wells. Yet, I see my story as small potatoes compared to the many other success stories in America.

I simply strived hard in my life to achieve success and prosperity and I achieved it at a level I am happy with. In America, with ambition, attitude, some basic skills and a little bit of luck, you can have both success and prosperity. It's possible to have success without prosperity and prosperity without success and I have to say that I consider myself more successful than prosperous because the contentment, good health, and happiness with a loving family I consider to be my greatest achievement.

I have set goals and maintained the tenacity to achieve many of them. I have remained positive in good times and in bad. Surrounding myself with good people, being decisive and taking carefully calculated risks has brought me my share of luck. Most importantly, I have had fun advancing in a very diversified career.

I'd like to tell young people who are struggling today, just like I did all those years ago, that finding their best skill and sticking with it will give them their best chance to succeed. I know that there are kids today facing some of the exact same challenges I faced. I know it because I've met them. In my experience of visiting Boys and Girls Clubs I have seen kids with backgrounds similar to mine. Time may have passed, but circumstances have not.

I would like to take the liberty here to toss in a touch of advice to young people on how to approach their jobs; their foundation for building a future. Look the part, act the part, be early, stick to it and finish right! Those principles apply to the application, on the job and the day you leave the job. And, they apply to every job. The most common and biggest mistake for workers is to consider the purpose of their job to be for the money only. Those who disrespect their job because they think they have better plans may never get to the better plans.

Look the part: Picture the image your employer would like and present yourself accordingly. Consider hair, hygiene, scent, posture, facial expression, voice, the way you walk and especially the way you dress.

Act the part: Stay busy, find work, be eager, never argue, communicate clearly, be humble, appreciate your job and show loyalty.

Be early: Show up on the job before your scheduled time and be first to volunteer where help is needed. Abbreviate your breaks.

Stick to it: Don't become complacent. Find extra work to do. Do more than you were asked to do. Observe and learn from those who are succeeding. Be prepared. Be patient.

Finish right: Complete every task in a positive manner and the best you know how. Value your future reference. Leave like you want to return. Leave with a smile and appreciation, regardless of the circumstances.

The same principles apply as you climb up the ladder. You now have to set the example, treat others fairly, select workers who want your job, know every aspect of your job and know your customer. In upper management you add creating teamwork, projecting positive results and staying on top of the numbers. As an owner you must take carefully calculated risk, know your market and create value.

One of the restaurant chains of which I am a franchisee, Taco Bell, provides national support to The Boys and Girls Club of America. Taco Bell-supported programs include gang prevention, facilities improvements, and various programs to encourage youth to become responsible citizens. The Boys and Girls Club is an organization that saves many young lives by providing young people with hope for the future and access to understanding leaders. That's why any profits I attain from the sales of this book will be donated to The Boys and Girls Club of America.

Wayne and Chef Herm at the Warwick Hills, 1965.

Terry with twin Cherri, 1946.

Terry and Wayne, 1962 wedding.

Wayne and Terry's family, 1971.
Jeff holding Greg, Marty and Cherri.

1987. L-r: front Greg, Jeff, Cherri. Back Marty, Terry, Wayne.

Cherri, Marty, Jeff, Greg at Jeff's wedding, 1993.

Grandchildren: Bottom L-r. Niam, Rowan, Aria, Jolie
Top L-r. Wayne, Dayne, Deacon, Terry

Wayne, right, with brother Gerald, 1993.

Wayne visiting Lavern in his cave in Boulder, Colorado, 2007.

Wayne and Terry on a cruise in Asia, 2006.

Lobdell Family Tree
(To the limited extent available)

Stephon Lobdell, 1467, England.
William, 1455-1527, England.
John, 1480-1453, England.
Nicholas, 1510-1546, immigrant from Devon—born Eastbourne, Sussex, England.
William, 1536-1580, England.
Nicholas, 1578-1650, England.
Simon Lobdell, 1632, came to America in 1635.
Joshua, 1671-1742, (Simon's only son), America.
Ebenezer, (with Joshua's first wife, Mary Burwell), America.
Ebenezer, Jr., America.
Thomas, America.
James, 1818-1894, First Sheriff of Muskegon County, Michigan in 1857.
    Wife: Ruby Ann Lewis.
    Sons: James, Chester, William, Ebenezer.
Chester, 1847-1894, farmer in western Michigan.
    Wife: Mary Mason.
Edward, 1875-1942, farmer.
    Wife: Martha Peterson.
    Sons: Chester, Alfred, Howard.
    Daughters: Hazel and Mary.
Howard, 1909-1984, farmer.
    Wife: Marion (Leiffers) DeWilder.
    Sons: Russell, Lavern, Gerald, Wayne.
Wayne, 1941, restaurant owner, business developer.
    Wife: Terry (Collinge) Lobdell, teacher, home maker.
    Sons: Wayne Jeffrey, Marty, Greg.
    Daughter: Cherri.
Wayne Jeffery, Michigan State graduate, owns restaurants.
    Sons: Dayne and Deacon, with wife Athena.
Martin Jerome Lobdell, J.D., MBA, Michigan, attorney, venture capital, hedge funds.
Cherri Ann (Lobdell) Malkani, Michigan State and Northwestern University.
    Husband: Sanjay Malkani
    Sons: Niam and Rowan, daughter, Aria.
Gregory Mathew Lobdell.
    Wife: Andi (Hancock).
    Daughter: Jolie Tru.

Some genealogy records provided by *John B. Mason, Mathews, NC and Starla Willea, Muskegon, Michigan.*

Wayne Lobdell, a multi-business developer and entrepreneur is semi-retired, enjoying summers in Traverse City, Michigan and winters in Hillsboro, Beach Florida. A graduate of Michigan State University, Wayne has developed real estate, restaurants, money management businesses, gas and oil and numerous venture capital projects. He divides his time between enjoying his family, business, writing and playing golf.

CPSIA information can be obtained at www.ICGtesting.com
Printed in the USA
240681LV00001B/6/P